Pastor Isaac Adams has written a book about important matters. What's more, it's a book that is true, good, simple and clear, filled with very practical advice for the new Christian. Some of this teaching is too rare today. And it is accompanied by a story with some surprising depth. All in all, a tool worth knowing about and using.

Mark Dever

Senior Pastor, Capitol Hill Baptist Church, Washington D.C.

This book on training for godliness is relevant for Christians not just in the West but also in the East. Thank you, brother for writing this book to help Christians to understand the importance of training for godliness. You have challenged believers to pursue godliness without falling into the trap of legalism. The readers will be spurred on to work hard to be more like Christ, leaning and trusting on the abundant grace available for us. This book will be encouraging for seasoned Christians as well as for new believers also. I pray that the Lord will use this book to help believers all over the world to grow in godliness and maturity.

Harshit Singh

Pastor, Satya Vachan Church (True Word Church), India

Many young believers are hungry for discipleship, yet they have been turned away by more mature saints with a dismissive 'I don't know how' or 'I don't have time.' This gap leaves young believers groping toward spiritual maturity through painful trial and error, longing for community, companionship, and wiser guidance. Isaac Adams' plainly spoken and biblically sound workbook interrupts the cycle of 'discipleship apathy,' and gives us ample skills in prayer, evangelism, church, community, and more. We all could use a refresher course in *Training*, and heed his exhortation to 'train for eternity' by helping each other live more wisely today.

K. A. Ellis

for the Study of the Bible and Ethnicity

Reformed Theological Seminary, Atlanta

We cannot force God to give us his grace, but we can position ourselves along the paths where he loves to give it. Let Isaac Adams be your guide to spiritual growth as a divine gift—and a calling for all who claim the name of Christ.

David Mathis

Executive Editor, desiringGod.org

Pastor, Cities Church, Minneapolis/St Paul

Author, *Habits of Grace: Enjoying Jesus through the Spiritual Disciplines*

IX 9Marks | First Steps Series

TRAINING

HOW DO I GROW AS A CHRISTIAN?

ISAAC ADAMS

SERIES EDITED BY MEZ McCONNELL

paperback ISBN 978-1-5271-0102-9
epub ISBN 978-1-5271-0500-3
mobi ISBN 978-1-5271-0501-0

10 9 8 7 6 5 4 3 2 1

Published in 2019
by
Christian Focus Publications Ltd,
Geanies House, Fearn, Ross-shire,
IV20 1TW, Great Britain.

www.christianfocus.com

Cover and interior design by Rubner Durais

Printed and bound
by Bell & Bain, Glasgow

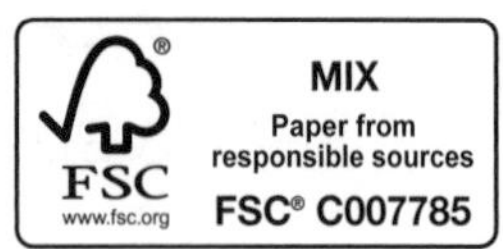

CONTENTS

To Avett Adams,
May you come to know Jesus,
and may you never recover.

PREFACE

I grew up with a pretty good life. I had both parents. I lived in an OK part of Washington, D.C. Yet the older I grew, the more I saw that brokenness doesn't care where you live. It comes for us all. It's in us all.

When it comes to knowing Jesus, my story is one where I could tell you the gospel before I believed it. I grew up thinking I was a Christian because I did, or tried to do, certain things. I went to church and read my Bible. I went to a Christian school and got good grades. None of this was bad on the surface, but under the surface was a bad heart. You see, though I knew about God, I didn't know God—and that became clear when I went to college. But that's also when God, in His mercy, brought my world crashing down. My pride got crushed. My family broke. But God also unplugged my ears. I heard the gospel preached, and I repented and trusted in Christ. I rejoiced, because I learned Christianity is more about what Jesus has *done*, not what I do.

In school, I studied journalism. I've always loved writing, and I love encouraging people to know Jesus. When I was asked to write this book, I thought it would be a good chance to do both—especially for people who know brokenness. That's mainly who the editors want this series of books to serve. A pastor once told me that when it comes to churches and Christian resources, 'The Hood always gets the leftovers.' So, I've tried to make this workbook a main meal for folks there. After all, if people, who are made in God's image, are broken and bleeding on the side of the road, Christians should help. Regardless of what neighborhood that road runs through, Christians should wisely and urgently love their neighbors. Of course, I can't save anybody—only Jesus can—so I pray this book helps you to know Him, not just about Him, as you train for eternity.

Before I finish this note, I've got to say one more thing because no one is self-made and neither is any book. I want to thank the friends who helped with this project and Capitol Hill Baptist Church, which has taught me so much. Megan, my dear wife, your patience with my writing amazes me. Words fail me at this point, so I'll stop with two: Thank you.

Romans 11:36

Isaac Adams
Washington, D.C.
2019

SERIES INTRODUCTION

The First Steps series will help equip those from an unchurched background take the first steps in following Jesus. We call this the 'pathway to service' as we believe that every Christian should be equipped to be of service to Christ and His church no matter your background or life experience.

If you are a church leader doing ministry in hard places, use these books as a tool to help grow those who are unfamiliar with the teachings of Jesus into new disciples. These books will equip them to grow in character, knowledge and action.

Or if you yourself are new to the Christian faith, still struggling to make sense of what a Christian is, or what the Bible actually says, then this is an easy to understand guide as you take your first steps as a follower of Jesus.

There are many ways to use these books.

- They could be used by an individual who simply reads through the content and works through the questions on their own.
- They could be used in a one-to-one setting, where two people read through the material before they meet and then discuss the questions together.
- They could be used in a group setting where a leader presents the material as a talk, stopping for group discussion throughout.

Your setting will determine how you best use this resource.

A USER'S KEY:

As you work through the studies you will come across the following symbols…

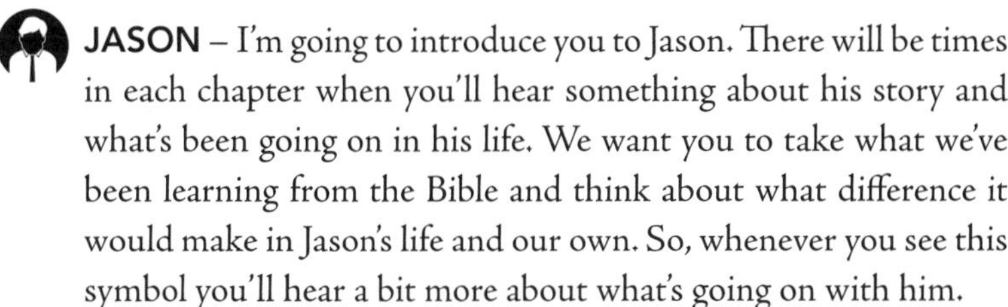

JASON – I'm going to introduce you to Jason. There will be times in each chapter when you'll hear something about his story and what's been going on in his life. We want you to take what we've been learning from the Bible and think about what difference it would make in Jason's life and our own. So, whenever you see this symbol you'll hear a bit more about what's going on with him.

ILLUSTRATION – Through real-life examples and scenarios, these sections help us to understand the point that's being made.

STOP – When we hit an important or hard point, we'll ask you to stop and spend some time thinking or chatting through what we've just learnt. This might be answering some questions, or it might be hearing more of Jason's story.

KEY VERSE – The Bible is God's Word to us, and therefore it is the final word to us on everything we are to believe and how we are to behave. Therefore we want to read the Bible first, and we want to read it carefully. So whenever you see this symbol you are to read or listen to the Bible passage three times. If the person you're reading the Bible with feels comfortable, get them to read it at least once.

MEMORY VERSE – At the end of each chapter we'll suggest a Bible verse for memorisation. We have found Bible memorisation to be really effective in our context. The verse (or verses) will be directly related to what we've covered in the chapter.

SUMMARY – Also, at the end of each chapter we've included a short summary of the content of that chapter. If you're working your way through the book with another person, this might be useful to revisit when picking up from a previous week.

MEET JASON

Jason is a young man who recently turned from his sins and trusted in Jesus, which is to say Jason recently became a Christian. His conversion to Christianity was an event—it only happened once. Yet Jason is realizing that, as John Stott said, '*becoming* a Christian is one thing; *being* a Christian is another.'[1] Jason is realizing that as a Christian, his whole life now revolves around Jesus. But if he's honest, he's not sure what this new life should look like. He used to go out and get drunk on weekends. Now he's wondering what Christians even do on Friday nights. He's asking, 'How do I grow as a Christian?'

1 John Stott, *Being a Christian* (Leicester: InterVarsity Press, 1957), p. 3.

INTRODUCTION: GET READY FOR TRAINING

In this book, we'll look at how the Bible says Christians should live and grow. **This book is about working for something.**

ILLUSTRATION

What does Michael Jordan have in common with an ant? What does basketball's biggest name share with one of nature's smallest creatures? Here's the answer: They both train for a certain outcome. Jordan ruthlessly practiced to be a great basketball player, and the ant puts in work for its food. The Bible says the ant shows what it looks like to work hard.

Go to the ant, O sluggard;
consider her ways, and be wise.
Without having any chief,
officer, or ruler,
she prepares her bread in summer
and gathers her food in harvest.
(Prov. 6:6-8)

We're not going to be talking about basketball training, though, or how hard bugs work, **and that's because this book is about training for godliness.**

A godly person is someone people can count on to be living as God commands Christians to live. The Bible commands good servants of Jesus to train to live this way.

'Train yourself for godliness' (1 Tim. 4:7).

STOP:

How does working to be godly sound to you?

We've got good coaches on our side to help us with our training. You may not know their names, but don't worry, you'll gain advice from wise Christian pastors and teachers, past and present.

But before we hear more from them, we need to remember one thing:

> **Christians don't live godly lives *to be* saved;**
>
> **they live godly lives because they *have been* saved.**

A godly life is always a result of salvation, never the way to earn salvation. This point is crucial because this book focuses on spiritual growth. When people focus on their spiritual growth, they're often tempted to think God will like them more if they're behaving better. Maybe you've heard people say, 'God helps those who help themselves.' While that phrase sounds awfully religious, it's actually an awful lie. That saying promises God will love you if you just clean up your act a bit. Yet the good news of Jesus—what's known as 'the gospel'—says something else.

The gospel says God, our creator, is so good that he won't overlook any sin. Sin is our rebellion against God, and we rebel because we, like all people, are born sinners (Rom. 3:23; Ps. 51:5).We could think of our problem like this:

Sin is the disease we are all born with, and the symptom is that we rebel against God.

Too often, we do, think, feel, say, and want what we want instead of what God wants. We're fully responsible for our sins and the gospel says all people are so sinful—so sick—that it's impossible for us to clean ourselves up enough for God. *We can't cure ourselves of our sickness.* We might seem like goody-two-shoes in front of our friends and families, maybe even in front of our mirrors. But so long as we're spiritually sick, we're sinners in front of our God.

We're under His judgment,

and we deserve to die

and suffer under His righteous wrath

forever.

This is the fair penalty for our sin.

But the gospel doesn't stop there, and it'd be really bad news if it did. The good news of Jesus really is good, though, because it says that God helps those who *can't* help themselves. He heals those who can't heal themselves. God has done that by

sending His Son Jesus

to live the life we should have lived

and die the death on the cross we deserved.

After His death, Jesus was raised by God from the dead so that anyone who trusts in Him for salvation and turns from their sins will be forgiven of their sins and given eternal life. This is the good news: 'By [Jesus'] wounds we are healed' (Isa. 53:5, NIV)! And God doesn't just stop with healing us; *He* causes *us* to grow up as spiritually healthy people. Praise God, He *commands* us to be godly and *helps* us to be godly!

'Work out your salvation with fear and trembling, for it is God who works in you to will and to act in order to fulfill his good purpose' (Phil. 2:12-13, NIV).

Friends, God's *grace trains* us (Titus 2:11-12). Any good work we do shows God's good work in us, and so we gratefully rely on His strength, not ours, and we give Him all the praise for our godliness.

The world says,

'God helps those who help themselves!'

The gospel says,

'God helps those who can't help themselves.'

So the message of this book isn't: 'Practice these Christian basics, and you'll be a better person.' The Christian's hope isn't that practice makes perfect, but that *Jesus makes perfect*. When *we trust in Jesus, God declares us innocent of all our sin*. He sees us as He sees Jesus—His perfect child.

Do you think this all sounds too good to be true? Some folks don't need the reminder that they can't earn God's love. They know they're sinful, but they think they're so sinful that God would never want them. But here's the problem with that kind of thinking: it still assumes God wants us because of us. Yet the Bible says God's love for us isn't based on us. Instead, God's love is based on His own free choice to love us (Deut. 7:7-9; Eph. 2:4-5). The gospel assures us His love is secured for us because of what Jesus has *done*, not because of what we *do*.

Do you see how through the gospel, **God offers hope** for *all kinds of people?*

He offers hope to those who think too highly of themselves—people who think they can reach up to God because of their good behavior.

Yet God also offers hope to those who think too lowly of themselves—people who think God would never reach down to them because of their bad behavior.

People who think too highly of themselves are often **perfectionists** who *worry too much about how perfectly they behave*. People who think too lowly of themselves are often **imperfectionists** who *worry too much about how imperfectly they behave.*

> **Perfectionists** often measure their relationship with God on how obedient they've been recently.
>
> **Imperfectionists** often feel worthless before God because they never stop looking at their failures, and they think God won't either.

But when we keep our eyes on Jesus, we keep our eyes on the very person who makes us acceptable before God. We no longer have to fear God's rejection, and that truth should encourage us to grow in godliness.

Remember 1 Timothy 4:7. It says godliness doesn't come without training (see also Heb. 5:14). Elsewhere in the Bible, when writing about training for godliness, Paul uses examples from sport. He says he practices

> like an athlete who disciplines himself,
>
> like a runner running a race (1 Cor. 9:24-27).

One of the main goals of that race is to become a mature Christian (Col. 1:28-29).

JASON

Even though he's an adult, Jason is a baby Christian. He's young in his faith, a beginner. And like anyone new at anything, Jason will have to get help from others, learn the basics, and practice them to figure out what he's trying to do. Some days this training may be tough. Some days, Jason may even want to quit. What's more, Jason, like the rest of us, still *wrestles with sin and weakness*. And if our sin wasn't enough, some of us are in harsh circumstances, which makes obeying God even more difficult (Exod. 6:9).

Indeed, like Michael Jordan, Jason is discovering there is no growth without pain and practice. As J.C. Ryle put it: 'There are no spiritual gains without pains.'[1]

But unlike Mike, Jason doesn't train for his greatness; he trains to know and enjoy more of God's greatness. And that makes training worth it because through training we get to enjoy God in this life—the very God who we'll enjoy forever in the next life. The Christian life is about many things, but in one major sense, it's about **getting ready for heaven**.

Ryle said, God placed us on earth '*to **train for eternity***.'[2]

What does that training look like? Our friend Jason is wondering just that.

1 J. C. Ryle, *Holiness* (Moscow, ID: Charles Nolan Publishers, 2001), p. 25.

2 J. C. Ryle, *Thoughts for Young Men* (Carlisle, PA: Banner of Truth, 2015), p. 43.

WHAT'S THE POINT?

Followers of Jesus love God and their neighbors.

1. DISCIPLESHIP: FOLLOWING JESUS

JASON

Jason didn't have much money growing up. When he was a kid, his dad left him, his older brother, and their mother—and he took their money with him. So Jason and his brother could never afford video games or fancy bikes. Nonetheless, they discovered they didn't need money to have fun. As they played with their neighborhood friend, Chip, they grew to love other games, especially 'Follow the Leader.' The game was free and easy. Someone was named the 'head' of a line, and everyone else had to follow the head and do what they did; if they didn't, they lost.

In this chapter, we're going to answer two questions. **The first question is 'What is a disciple?'** The game Jason played as a child points to an answer: *A disciple is someone who follows their leader.* To be a disciple of Jesus is to be a follower of Jesus.

A disciple is a follower.

While Jason's childhood game gave us a basic picture of a disciple, let's also consider what the Bible says about being a disciple. After all, we don't want to only think in a basic way but a *biblically* basic way.

STOP:

What do you think it looks like to follow Jesus?

Looking at the Bible, Carl Ellis, Jr., defined being a disciple of Jesus like this: **'A disciple is someone in the process of learning to obey all things Christ commands.'**[1] In other words, a disciple is a student. This definition comes from Jesus' final instructions to His disciples. In Matthew 28:18-20, Jesus said:

'All authority in heaven and on earth has been given to me. Therefore go and make disciples of all nations, baptizing them in the name of the Father and of the Son and of the Holy Spirit, and teaching them to obey everything I have commanded you. And surely I am with you always, to the very end of the age.' (NIV)

With these words, Jesus was saying to His disciples: 'I'm the leader. Go and make more disciples and teach them to follow me as I've commanded you to follow me.' Since being a disciple requires learning from other disciples, no one can be a disciple all by themselves. A solo disciple is a contradiction in terms.

A disciple is a student.

JASON

Jason has found that though following Jesus is personal, it's not private. In fact, following Jesus is a pretty public thing. Just as there are no solo disciples, there are also no secret disciples. Disciples are meant to show what God is like. We're meant to be billboards you can see, not ninjas you can't.

Jason is learning about following Jesus publicly. He's known old Ms. Pearl for a long time. She was his family's neighbor growing up, and she owns a store in the neighborhood. Though Jason always went to church with his mother, Marie, Ms. Pearl treats Jason differently now that he's a Christian. When she sees him

1 Carl Ellis Jr, <https://twitter.com/CarlEllisJr/status/931142058353549312>. Date accessed: 5th July 2019.

in the hallway, she gently grabs his wrist and asks him, 'Young brother, are you encouraged in the Lord?'

'Uh, I think so,' Jason usually answers, unsure what old Ms. Pearl means.

'Then that's a win,' Ms. Pearl would respond before hobbling off.

Some of the guys Jason is getting to know at church, like Eddy, even ask him questions about his sin, and Jason's slightly embarrassed to answer. They never ask to embarrass him, but the questions still feel like spiritual shovels digging into Jason's dirt.

On top of all this, Jason's friends and family, who aren't Christians, keep asking him why he doesn't do some of the things he used to do. Some friends, like Chip, ask because they really want to know what's caused this change. Jason following Jesus seems weird but attractive to Chip. He can't describe it, but Jason's new life has a different smell to it, and he likes it. Chip has even seen how Eddy treats Jason, and that's struck him.

'I don't know how God treats people,' Chip said to Jason, 'but I feel like it'd be how Eddy treats you.'

Jason's brother, on the other hand, is Alexander; Chip and Jason always called him Alex for short and Al for shorter. Al tried Christianity as a kid, but now he basically hates it. He used to ask Jason about following Jesus, but not in a serious way: 'Hey, how's your new wife Jesus?' Al would ask, mocking Jason's new life. Al wants the old Jason back, not this new guy. Unlike Chip, Al thinks Jason's obedience to Jesus smells like death, and he wants nothing to do with it. In fact, Al has even begun to ignore Jason.

All Christians have to learn the basic lessons Jason is learning. So this book is divided into two parts:

Personal Training

and

Public Training

In the first part, we'll look at habits a disciple of Jesus individually practices to train for godliness, and in the second part, we'll look at habits disciples practice with other people to train for godliness. The habits we form to train for godliness are often called spiritual disciplines.[2]

We're starting with personal training because the Christian life begins with a personal choice to follow Jesus. Plus, it's hard to help others do something if you're not doing it yourself.

ILLUSTRATION

A lifeguard can't save anyone if he doesn't know how to swim. The same is true of Christians: we should follow Jesus before we help others do the same.

Do we have to know everything or be perfect before we teach others? Not at all. Does that mean we have an excuse then to not help others? Not at all. We should simply follow Jesus before we lead others to do the same.

But let's say Jason gets that point, and he's still left wondering, **'What does it actually look like to obey all that Jesus has commanded?'** That's our second question in this chapter. It might sound overwhelming to think about obeying *all* of Jesus' commandments. Jason isn't even really sure where to find them all, and that's okay. Remember, he's a beginner!

---

2 Some Christians prefer the term 'means of grace' instead of 'spiritual disciplines' to reflect the fact that *God's work* in us is what matters most for our godliness.

Christians find all that Jesus commanded in the Bible, and Jesus has been kind enough to summarize what God requires of us into two basic commands:

'You shall love the Lord your God with all your heart and with all your soul and with all your mind. This is the great and first commandment. And a second is like it: You shall love your neighbor as yourself' (Matt. 22:36-39).

These two commands will be our focus for the rest of this chapter. **What does it look like for disciples to obey all that Christ has commanded? It looks like loving your God and loving your neighbor.** If Jason is going to train to follow Jesus, he must—relying on God's grace—work hard to do those two things.

JESUS' DISCIPLES LOVE GOD

Through reading the Bible and hearing it taught at church, Jason is slowly learning that when God talks about love, He pretty much means the opposite of what the world means. The world tells us love looks like rainbows, feels like butterflies in our tummies, and comes easy, fast, and free.

But the Bible tells us love can be

hard,

slow work,

and in this world,

love can hurt.

After all, consider Jesus' crucifixion: how loving, and yet how hard, messy, and painful. The world says love is a feeling that focuses on ourselves—how happy we are, how happy things or people make us. And though God cares deeply about our happiness, Jason is learning that God ought to be at the center of it.

JASON

Jason is beginning to understand that a disciple's love for God is seen most clearly by whether or not they obey God out of gratitude for what he's done for them. Jesus says, 'Anyone who loves me will obey my teaching' (John 14:23, NIV).

But there's a problem: Jason disobeys Jesus sometimes because like every Christian, he still sins. And so, like *every Christian,* Jason needs *to regularly repent.*

Jesus commands everyone to do this spiritual discipline called repentance:

'Jesus began to preach, saying, "Repent, for the kingdom of heaven is at hand"' (Matt. 4:17).

Repentance is turning from sin and to God. Spiritually speaking, repentance is...

walking one way and

turning around to walk the other way.

Repentance is a transfer of allegiance—a repentant person allies with Jesus instead of their sin. Repentance is the other side of the coin of faith. According to God's Word, faith isn't sitting back and hoping for the best. It's not blind trust. Rather, faith is being confident in our hope as Christians and certain of what we don't see (Heb. 11:1). It's being confident in God and His promises, and this confidence leads us to action. One of those essential actions is repentance.

JASON

Jason repented when he became a Christian; he turned *from* his sin and turned *to* Jesus in faith. However, though Jason only became a Christian once, he's learning that repentance isn't just a one-time event. It's a regular part of the Christian life.

A famous Bible teacher named Martin Luther said: 'When our Lord and Master Jesus Christ said, "Repent" in Matthew 4, he willed the entire life of believers to be one of repentance.'[3] To put it differently, **repenting is what God's people do in this life.** Jason won't repent of every single sin he ever commits. No Christian sees sin that clearly.

But Jason still wonders, *what does repentance look like practically?* Here's one answer: Confession.

STOP:

What is repentance? How often do Jesus' disciples repent? What sins in your life do you need to repent of?

By confession, the Bible doesn't mean you must sit in a booth and talk to a priest. The Bible means we admit our sins to God and ask His forgiveness. We'll think more about how to do this in the chapter on prayer.

For now, it needs to be said that true confession isn't simply saying sorry and moving on with life. True confession isn't just being sad that our sins got us into some kind of trouble, and now we have to deal with the consequences. That kind of regret is what the Bible calls 'worldly grief.' True confession, on the other hand, is marked by *godly grief*—which is genuinely being sad that our sins offend God. The Bible says worldly grief leads us to life *apart* from God. Godly grief leads us to life *with* God.

'For godly grief produces a repentance that leads to salvation without regret, whereas worldly grief produces death.' (2 Cor. 7:10)

Rather than death, the gospel offers Christians hope:

---

3 Martin Luther, '95 Theses.' <https://reformed.org/historic-confessions/the-95-theses-by-martin-luther/>. Date accessed: 9th July 2019.

If we confess our sins,

no matter what sin we commit,

we can count on God to forgive us

because Jesus already took God's wrath for us on the cross.

The penalty for our sins before God is death and hell. But Jesus paid the debt we owed God for our sins, and because God is always fair, He'll never ask us to pay Him something we no longer owe. The Bible reminds us of this:

'If we confess our sins, [God] is faithful and just to forgive us our sins and to cleanse us from all unrighteousness.' (1 John 1:9)

When Jason confesses his sin, he's showing that he trusts God to keep this great promise. He's admitting that *he's a great sinner,* but he's admitting with hope, since he knows *God is a greater forgiver.* When Jason confesses his sin, he's admitting that God knows everything, so it's silly to try and hide from Him.

JASON

Jason remembered a time he tried to hide sin from God. He had gone into Ms. Pearl's store, and he gave her a big hug. But he hugged her to distract her, so that Chip and Al could steal some food behind her back. The boys left the store like nothing happened. As they walked down the street, they celebrated, looking at the grub they stole, thinking they got away with it. Jason looked up, however, and saw something—an old church building off the side of the road. The building had beautiful stained glass windows; they reflected lots of colors and history. But they didn't reflect much about what's going on *inside* that church. For all Jason knew at the time, that church could be teaching lies. After all, stained glass is meant to be looked at, not through.

Jason realized that how he treated Ms. Pearl was like those stained glass windows—his hug was beautiful on the outside, but hid an ugly heart on the inside. Even though no one else can, God can see through our stained glass. After Jason became a Christian, he confessed his sin to Ms. Pearl, and she did the oddest thing. Instead of taking him to the police, she gave him some food for free. She showed him mercy, by sparing him of something he *did* deserve—punishment. And then she showed him grace, by giving him something he *didn't* deserve—food from her store. For Christians, that's how our merciful and gracious God treats us.

Yet Jason wasn't finished confessing when he confessed to Ms. Pearl. He needed to also confess to God because **all sin is against God**. So Jason confessed to God in prayer and asked for His forgiveness. When Jason did that, he shattered the stained glass and showed what's really going on inside his heart.

When Jason confessed his sin, he agreed with God's judgment. He's begun turning from sin and turning to God.

It's true that **repentance requires more than confession**—it requires that we **fight our sin**, not only confess it. It requires that

we change what we want,

how we behave,

and whom we're trusting in.

Again, we need God's help for this, which is why the Psalm writer asked God to create a new heart in him (Ps. 51:10). We need God's help because **repentance** isn't a *mere fix to bad behavior;* **it's a change in heart** that leads *to a changed life*. Only God can change hearts!

True repentance requires nothing *less* than confession, and as a new disciple, Jason must begin here. As Jason trains through regular confession and repentance, he will—with God's help—grow in hatred of sin because he's growing to love God with all he's got. This is the first and greatest commandment.

JESUS' DISCIPLES LOVE THEIR NEIGHBORS

'And a second [command] is like it,' Jesus said, *'You shall love your neighbor as yourself.'* Jesus commanded His disciples to love God *and* their neighbors. When Jason heard that command, he wondered, 'Who's my neighbor?' A lawyer once asked Jesus that same question.

In Luke 10:30-37, Jesus answered that question with the Parable of the Good Samaritan. He described a man who was beaten up and left for dead; the Bible says the man was 'half-dead.' You would think the really religious people who saw the man would help him, but they walked past him. However, another person came close to the man, and it was someone the man wouldn't have expected or respected; it was someone the man would've thought of as an enemy. But instead of coming to *hurt* the half-dead man; the enemy came to *serve* him.

Unlike the religious people who walked by the half-dead man, the enemy took care of him. Jesus used the half-dead man's enemy as a picture for what it looks like to be someone's neighbor. He commands everyone to go and be like this good neighbor.

STOP:

Who is someone in your life who you think of as an enemy? When that person comes to mind, how do you feel? What would it look like to love them?

What does this story have to do with being a disciple of Jesus? In answering the lawyer's question, Jesus showed that to love our neighbor means to love people, and that includes loving our enemies. Who among us has done that perfectly? The lawyer who asked Jesus the question didn't, Jason knows he hasn't, and Jason knows that means he doesn't deserve heaven.

Apart from Jesus, Jason is just as doomed as that lawyer. None of us has loved like the unexpected neighbor in Jesus' story. It's impossible to obey Jesus' command to go and be like that neighbor because of our sin. The good news, however, is that Jesus perfectly kept that command, and he did even more than that. Jesus loved His enemies by dying for them on the cross—by dying for us if we trust in Him.

'While we were enemies we were reconciled to God by the death of his Son.' (Rom. 5:10)

Every disciple of Jesus used to be an enemy of Jesus, but **Jesus has restored our relationship with God**. And yet, being restored to God doesn't mean His commands don't matter for us anymore. *God's commands teach us how to live.* We should obey them, and if we're growing as Christians we'll want to obey them.

Jesus commands His disciples to love their neighbors, and in the story of the half-dead man, **Jesus showed us what this love looks like**:

It looks like kindness, justice, and mercy.

It looks like stooping down to people,

not turning our noses up at them.

It looks like working for our neighbor's good,

even if our neighbor works for our bad.

It looks like going near people whom the world would walk away from

and spending time on people whom the world would ignore.

This love means not treating someone like a problem just because they have a problem. This love means putting other people's desires before our own. This love means going *through* trouble if it means getting our neighbor *out of* trouble.

What does a disciple's love for their neighbor look like? Ultimately, it looks a lot like God's love for us. The more we know God's love for us, the more we'll love our enemies and neighbors.

No doubt, this love will look different depending on the situation. Yet there's one situation we should be clear about, and that's *when your enemy is abusing you*. Maybe it's a spouse, another family member, or an authority figure. Whoever it is, let's be clear that what the abuser is doing is an offence to God, and it's not your fault.

> **If you're being abused, know that kindness and mercy toward your abuser does not look like staying in a dangerous situation. *Please talk to someone you trust so they can help you.***

JASON

Jason is learning that this kind of love is hard. It requires forgiving his father who abandoned him. It requires forgiving his brother, Al, who mocks him. Nonetheless, Jason is starting to see that as he follows Jesus, his life is looking more like Jesus'. Jesus had people He loved leave and betray Him, and now Jason has some, too.

God calls Christians not only to believe in Jesus, but also to 'suffer for his sake' (Phil. 1:29; 2 Tim. 1:8). It's tempting to think being a disciple of Jesus should be easy. But the Bible seems to suggest the opposite: Following Jesus is hard, and if it's not, something is probably off. That doesn't mean life can't be enjoyable. But until heaven, the Christian life is one of joy *and* sorrow (2 Cor. 6:10). Many people who call themselves preachers will say that Jesus came to make His disciples rich and free from pain or suffering in this life. **If anyone is telling you that—run the other way—because wherever they got that idea from, they didn't get it from the Bible.**

After all, Jesus didn't lead an easy life, and His ended on a cross. **And if we're going to follow Jesus as our leader**, we have to do what He says and *take up our own crosses.*

He said to all, 'If anyone would come after me, let him deny himself and take up his cross daily and follow me' (Luke 9:23).

By 'take up your cross,' Jesus means following Him is a kind of death because we give up what we want if it's not what He wants. As Richard Chin put it, 'Carrying our cross means that we, as Jesus' disciples, think it's better to die than to disobey Jesus. So disciples think it's better to die than to steal; it's better to die than to _______________(insert whatever sin you struggle with).'[4]

Despite all this talk about death, Jason is beginning to see following Jesus leads to life, just as He promised (Matt. 16:25). Despite some hard days, Jason sees that life with Jesus is tougher, but better. Jason has a peace no one can take from him, even scoffers like Al. And so Jason wants to follow God's Word more and more. He doesn't get it right every time, but he wants to know it more and more. That's the discipline we want to look at next—spending time with God—specifically by reading His Word.

MEMORY VERSE

'He said to all, "If anyone would come after me, let him deny himself and take up his cross daily and follow me"' (Luke 9:23).

---

4 Richard Chin, 'Seeing Jesus Properly: The Lord to Gladly Obey Forever', CROSS Conference, Kentucky International Convention Center, Dec. 27–30, 2013.

SUMMARY

In this chapter, we learned that a disciple is someone in the process of learning to obey all that Jesus commands—which, in summary, means to love God and our neighbor. We don't always do that, so a normal part of Christian life is confessing sin as we begin to repent of it, turning to the God who died for His enemies.

WHAT'S THE POINT?

Followers of Jesus read the Bible, a unique and useful book.

2. BIBLE: LISTENING TO GOD

(PART 1)

JASON

Jason has few memories of his father. Of course, he knew the man was selfish. What kind of father abandons his family and takes their money? But at the same time, Jason didn't really *know* his father, and that always left him a bit sad.

Jason's mother, Marie, did her best to fill the hole Jason's dad left. She worked long hours to put food on the table. Sometimes she would make it home before Jason went to sleep, and she'd sing him songs about Jesus as Jason drifted off. But often Jason sat home alone—for bedtime and for meals.

Lunch was never a problem, of course, because most days Jason ate at school. He'd sit in his typical place with his typical crew—with Chip on his left and Al his right. Sandwiched in the middle, Jason later realized that the sandwich his crew made up was better than any sandwich their school could afford to feed them, and he was OK with that. The boys never had much, but they had each other, and that was enough to make them kings of the sloppy, loud cafeteria.

But dinners at home were hard because Jason usually ate by himself. As a child, he'd often look at the empty chair where his mother would sit, if she could join him, and wonder what it would be like if his dad sat there instead. If he showed up, even for one night, what would they talk about? What kind of food would he like? Would he ever tell a joke, and would it be funny? Everyone knows at least one good joke, right?

It's been decades since those lonely dinners, and Jason now realizes that what saddens him isn't so much that his father never spent money on him; what saddens him is that his father never spent time with him. Jason never got to know his father. After all, how else can you get to know your father besides talking to him and listening to him?

The same goes for God. As a Christian, Jason is now one of God's children, and he'll get to know his Father by spending time with Him and listening to Him. However, unlike Jason's earthly father, Jason's heavenly Father will never leave him. God promises as much:

'I will never leave you nor forsake you.'

Where did Jason find that promise? He found it in the Bible, in Hebrews 13:5. He heard the preacher at church talking about it, and it stuck with him.

The next two chapters focus on reading the Bible because reading the Bible isn't optional for Christians; it's basic. It's vital. A Christian who tries to grow in godliness without reading the Bible is like a plant that tries to grow without water and light. Bible reading is a crucial aspect of a disciple's training. Why? Two reasons.

First, the Bible is a unique book. The Bible reveals

what God is like

and

what He likes,

and

there's no book like it.

Every other book, including this one, is imperfect; **the Bible is perfect.** It is truth (John 17:17). Every other book is written only by people; **the Bible is ultimately written by God** (2 Tim. 3:16). The Bible, or 'God's Word,' is **God talking to people.** Just as we speak to someone when we write them a letter, **God speaks to people through His Word.** So disciples like Jason read their Bibles to know God better.

If Jason wants to see what God says,

all he has to do is read his Bible.

Many people feel like they've never heard from God, and they assume that if He's real they would have. These folks may even beg God to speak to them, to show them a mighty sign, but all the while their Bibles are covered in dust. They don't read God's Word. They don't read about the signs already done or about people who begged for a sign instead of a savior (Matt. 16:4; John 12:37).

By God's grace, Jason has dusted off his Bible. And the more Jason reads it, the more he notices how much God's Word says about, well, God's Word.

- **God calls His Word a *fire and hammer* (Jer. 23:29)** *'Is not my word like fire, declares the LORD, and like a hammer that breaks the rock in pieces?'* God's Word has power. It has the power to give off heat and warm our cold hearts so that we can embrace God's truth. It has the power to break hearts of stone so that we can accept the truth.
- **God calls His Word a *sword* (Eph. 6:17)** *'take ... the sword of the Spirit, which is the word of God.'* Disciples defend

themselves from temptation to sin and the devil's lies with the sword of God's Word. In Hebrews 4:12, God even says that His Word is sharper than a sword, and because it is, it alone can pierce hearts with the truth.

- **God calls his Word a *light* (Ps. 119:105)** *'Your word is a lamp to my feet and a light to my path.'* God's Word guides us. *Without God's Word, we would be lost and headed the wrong way.* With God's Word, we can see the truth in this dark world.

- **God calls His Word *milk* (1 Pet. 2:2).** *'Like newborn infants, desire the pure milk of the word, so that you may grow up into your salvation'* (CSB) When a baby comes into the world, it can't fend for itself. It needs to be fed, and the main thing a parent feeds a baby is milk. Likewise, as Christians we can't fend for ourselves. Rather our Father feeds us His Word, nourishing our faith. God's Word keeps us healthy and thriving. Jason knows what it's like to miss a meal and suffer. If we didn't eat food for a couple of days, we'd begin to wither. The same goes for our souls if we neglect the food of God's Word. Jesus knew this. In Matthew 4, He quotes Deuteronomy 8:3 when Satan tempted Him. Jesus knew that physical food isn't ultimately what we need to survive; what we most need is God's Word.

Do you see from the verses above how God's Word is *unlike* any letter we could ever write? **The Bible is a unique book**, and Christians should treat it as such.

JASON

Once at University, Jason took a class about the Bible, which an atheist taught. A lot of Christians took the class. However, the professor asked the students on the first day how many of them had read the Harry Potter series. Lots of hands shot up. He then asked the students to keep their hands raised if they had read the entire Bible. Lots of hands went down.

'So,' the professor said, "The book you believe was written by the person who put planets in the sky—you haven't read it? Interesting.' Though he rejected God, that professor got the point: If the Bible is what God says it is, it's a book unlike any other.

In 2 Timothy 3:16, God says His Word is *'breathed out by God and profitable for teaching, for reproof, for correction, and for training in righteousness.'* Did you catch that? God Himself says the Bible is useful for our training.

STOP:

In what ways is the Bible like other books or letters you've read? In what ways is it different? How have you seen the power of God's Word in your life?

Here's the second reason the Bible is useful for our training: **Jesus tells us all He commands in the Bible.** Remember, a disciple is someone who is learning to obey all of what Jesus has commanded. The more we read the Bible, the more we find instructions for how we should train for godliness, and these instructions are part of all that Jesus has commanded us to obey.

JASON

Growing up, Jason, Chip, and Al never really understood what the Bible was. Al thought it was a bunch of religious stories, or a rulebook. Chip would joke that it explained how the dinosaurs went extinct. But now, like all disciples who regularly read the Bible, Jason is finding that it's so much more. He's seeing that though there are rules in the Bible, they're not rules to keep Jason *from* joy; these rules lead Jason *to* joy. Like a good parent who commands their kid to stay away from a hot stove, God gives rules for our good.

Typically, people think the Bible is a bunch of rules because they think they have to keep a bunch of rules to be a good person. When they find they can't keep these rules, they say the rules have crushed them. That's why so *many people think God's Word is 'oppressive.'* Jason knows he can't always keep God's rules. He knows he's not a good person. But he rejoices because the Bible says Jesus was crushed for us, so that we could be free—free to live according to what Jesus commanded in the Bible.

Our training begins with God's Word, and we begin there because God's Word began everything. God spoke creation into being. Just look at Genesis 1, and note how many times it repeats the phrase, 'God said.' Not only did God's Word begin creation, it also began *new* creation. The Bible says Christians are new creations:

'Therefore, if anyone is in Christ, he is a new creation. The old has passed away; behold, the new has come.' (2 Cor. 5:17)

Remember, there was an old version of Jason before he was a Christian. Now that Jason has trusted in Christ, there's a new version of him—the version some of his friends, like Al, don't like. How did this new Jason come about? It came about because Jason heard God's Word. When he heard it, it pierced his heart; it removed the scales from his eyes so he could see the truth. In short, the Bible gave Jason faith—that's what God's Word does, just as it says:

'So faith comes from hearing, and hearing through the word of Christ.' (Rom. 10:17; see also James 1:18)

As a new creation, Jason has been saved from God's wrath. To be sure, he's not yet been finally freed from sin in his heart and mind, which means his mind needs to be renewed (Rom. 12:2). One major way God renews our mind is through His Word. Here's one way we could think of that renewal process.

ILLUSTRATION

Imagine Jason's mind is a glass that has dirt stuck in the bottom of it.

> We want to clean the glass, but the dirt has been packed in there for years; it's dry and hard to get out. So we can't just turn the cup over and pour the dirt out.
>
> Here's how we clean the glass: We pour clean water into it. The more the clean water goes in, the more the dirt will go out. Eventually, the glass will overflow, and the dirt will begin to flow out.
>
> The same goes for our minds—**we need the milk of God's Word to clean our minds and grow us.** We won't ever clean our minds perfectly before heaven, but we should strive to keep cleaning them through God's Word.

We've seen that God's Word began creation, new creation, and it renews our minds. God's Word also *sustains* everything. Hebrews 1:3 says Jesus holds up the universe by the word of His power. This is the joy of reading the Bible—we come to know our Lord and Savior better! The only reason this book is in your hands and you yourself aren't falling apart into oblivion is because Jesus is holding all things together.

Practically, how do these truths train disciples? How can we not only see what God's Word *says*, but what it *means*? In the next chapter, we'll see how Jason answers practical questions like these. For now, we'll end this chapter by answering a question many people struggle with when they begin reading the Bible: **'Where should I start?'** Should we just close our eyes, open our Bibles, and read whatever page we land on?

You could, but here are five suggestions to begin your Bible reading wisely:

1. **Start reading *the gospel of Mark*.** This book is simple and especially good for new Christians. Start with a few verses a day and enjoy.

2. **Start reading with *your pastor*.** We'll talk about this in chapter six, but every **Christian should join a church**. One helpful way to read the Bible is to read whatever passage your preacher is preaching on. Some churches list the sermon schedule ahead of time. If your church doesn't, ask your preacher what he's preaching on the next week. If he doesn't know what he's preaching, look at what he's preached in the past. See if there's an archive of old sermons online. Whether the sermons are from the past or present, reading the Bible like this allows you to hear how a more mature Christian (your pastor) thinks through the Bible. And if you can read the text for upcoming sermons, your heart will be that much more ready to receive the meal of God's Word.

3. **Start reading with *a King*.** There are 30 or 31 days in a month, except for February. There are 31 Proverbs written by King Solomon. Why not read a chapter of Proverbs a day? If it's the third day of the month, read Proverbs 3. If it's the 24th day of the month, read Proverbs 24. This is a wonderful habit to develop. The Proverbs are practical, and clearly instruct Christians about how to live. Read alongside King Solomon, and your Bible diet will be full of wisdom.

4. **Start reading with *an older Christian*.** Ask an older Christian what they're reading, and see if they'd be willing to show you how they study the Bible. Maybe they'll even be willing to start reading the Bible with you. Ask your pastor if there's anyone in the church who'd be happy to read along with you.

5. **Start reading with *a Bible reading plan*.** There are different plans that get you through different portions of the Bible

at different speeds. You can find Bible plans online; your pastor can likely point you to one. There's no one plan that's necessarily better than others. If you're being helped to follow Jesus by however you read the Bible—keep reading the Bible that way. As the saying goes, 'if it ain't broke, don't fix it.'

Bible plans have clear benefits: They provide direction. They bring you to parts of the Bible you might not otherwise read or hear taught. They can show the Bible's connections in ways you may not have seen otherwise. Yet a warning is in order: It's possible to bite off more than you can chew with a reading plan, and sometimes people get more overwhelmed than helped by them. It's been said, 'Shoot for the moon. Even if you miss it, you'll land among the stars.' While that sounds inspiring, a new Christian might shoot to read the whole Bible and land among food regulations in Leviticus. Of course, the Mosaic Law teaches us about God. But if you're not sure where to start your Bible reading, the depths of its ethnic demands under the Old Covenant may not be the best place to begin.

Whatever you do—**start reading.** Hang in there and stick at it.

ILLUSTRATION

If you've ever flown on an airplane, they talk about how if the oxygen masks drop down, oxygen is flowing even if the mask doesn't inflate. The same is true of our Bible reading. Even if you can't see anything happening, oxygen is flowing. Read the Bible, and breathe in the Word of life.

MEMORY VERSE

'Like newborn infants, desire the pure milk of the word, so that you may grow up into your salvation.' (1 Pet. 2:2 CSB)

SUMMARY

Reading the Bible is an invaluable habit for Christians because the Bible is unlike any other book, and Jesus tells us all He commands in the Bible. In the Bible, we learn what God is like and what He likes. The Bible is perfect, powerful, and useful for our training in righteousness.

WHAT'S THE POINT?

Followers of Jesus can read the Bible with the P.O.I.A. method.

3. LISTENING TO GOD

(PART 2)

JASON

Eddy has become a spiritual mentor to Jason. He's teaching Jason how to follow Jesus, and he's beginning with how to read the Bible.

'I get that I should read it,' Jason told Eddy. 'I kind of have no idea how to, though. I just figured out where to even start reading.'

'That's OK!' Eddy said. 'We all start somewhere.'

Eddy went on to teach Jason the P.O.I.A. method of Bible reading: **Pray, Observe, Interpret, and Apply**. This isn't the only way to faithfully read God's Word, but many disciples have benefitted from it.

WHEN THEY READ THE BIBLE, DISCIPLES PRAY...

The writer of Psalm 119 prays a simple prayer as he reads God's Word: *'Open my eyes, that I may behold wondrous things out of your law.'* The writer recognizes that he needs God's help if he's going to understand God's Word, so he asks for it. We'll come back to prayer in our next chapter, but for now we should note that it's a good practice to come to God in prayer before we come to His Word. It shows that our hearts are humble, as we recognize our need, and it shows our hearts are hungry. And so we ask, much like a child who asks her parents for food.

WHEN THEY READ THE BIBLE, DISCIPLES OBSERVE...

Whenever we read the Bible, one of the first questions we should ask is: 'What does it say?' This may seem obvious, but the obvious questions are often the most important questions, and they're often the ones we skip over. To figure out what a passage says, we should ask questions like:

- *What does the passage say about God?*
- *What does it say about people and their need for God?*
- *What does it say about sin?*
- *What does it say about Jesus? How does the passage point to Jesus?*
- *Does the passage instruct me about how I should live? If so, how?*

There's no specific order we have to follow when asking these questions. That said, I began this list with a question about God because it's so easy to focus on ourselves when we read the Bible. We're naturally prone to forget that the Bible is *God's* letter. It's about God first and foremost, not us.

Of course, no one can answer these questions by just reading a passage once. The **key to observing** is to read, re-read, and read the passage again.

Keep your nose in it.

Read it out loud.

Mark repeated words.

If your Bible has cross-references, look them up. See who's speaking and why. To do any of this, you must **read, re-read, and read again**!

WHEN THEY READ THE BIBLE, DISCIPLES INTERPRET...

If observing is asking, 'What does the passage *say?*' then interpreting is asking, 'What does the passage *mean?*'

ILLUSTRATION

If my daughter was running out the door, and I said, 'Hold your horses!' she wouldn't think I want her to literally hold animals that gallop and have hooves, and I'd be an odd dad if I did. Instead, she'd understand that despite what I *said*, what I *meant* is that she needs to stop and be patient.

We want to understand what God *says* in His Word and also what He *means*. Otherwise, we might miss what our heavenly Father wants to say to us because we're too busy holding horses.

One helpful way to see what a passage means is by looking closely at its context. **Context is what comes before and after a passage.** It helps to know where you are in the story.

> **Without context, anyone can make the Bible say anything.**
>
> **Without context, it's difficult to understand the author's main point and how his original audience would have heard it, and so it's difficult to know how we should hear it.**

Context is one of the most helpful guardrails to keep us on the road of reading the Bible in ways God meant it to be read. It's been said the three most important rules for reading the Bible are

1) context,

2) context,

3) context,

The disciple of Jesus would do well to remember these rules.

Follow these three tips to get the context of a passage:

- *Learn what the verses before and after the passage say.* Read the chapter that comes before and after the passage. The more of the surrounding passages you read, the better you'll understand your passage.

- *Learn the overall point of the book your passage is in.* For example, John tells us why he wrote his book: so people would believe in Jesus (John 20:31). Knowing *why* John wrote helps us to understand *what* he wrote. Figuring out the point of a book can be tricky, but there are tools like Study Bibles that can help. Ask your pastor to help you find a reliable Bible commentary—one that summarizes things, so you can easily grasp the context, context, context.

- *Learn the genre of the passage.* A genre is a kind of something. People talk about different kinds of music—hip-hop, R & B, country, etc. We expect different types of music in these different genres. The same is true for the Bible; **different genres have different rules when it comes to interpretation.** Poetry is different than narrative, and narrative is different than prophecy, and so on. Study Bibles can help you learn genres, and so can your pastor. If you're stuck, ask him for help.

WHEN THEY READ THE BIBLE, DISCIPLES APPLY...

So we've prayed, asking for God's help in reading the Bible. We've observed, asking what the passage says as we've read and re-read it. We've interpreted, asking what the passage means, but we have one more step—we need to ask what it means *for us*.

In James 1:22, the Bible commands us: 'Be doers of the word, and not hearers only, deceiving yourselves.' In other words, when you hear God's Word, don't just listen to it and then do whatever you want. Instead, listen to it and do what God wants. Love God by putting what you've heard into action. That's what obedience is—love for God in action. And we get to that action by asking the question, 'What does this passage mean for me? How can I take the truth and apply it to my life?'

Why does applying the truth matter so much? Consider the example of Judas.

Jesus called Judas to be one of His disciples, and Judas followed Jesus for years. Thomas Goodwin said, 'Judas heard all of Christ's sermons.'[1] He literally heard God speak, but he didn't apply what he heard; instead, he betrayed Jesus. Judas shows us that hearing God's Word isn't enough to make us one of God's people. It has to be believed, and believing leads to doing, to applying.

So, let's say that Jason hears Jesus' command to love his enemies. He's prayed about it, thought about it, and thinks he knows what Jesus means, but what does that command mean *for Jason?* It means Jason ought to love Al. Despite how Al treats him, Jason ought to seek Al's good and not be bitter but kind to him. This love will be tough and may take a long time, but that's okay. After all, disciples are works-in-progress.

STOP:

Turn to Matthew 5:27-30. Pray before you read the passage, and then answer these questions:

1) What does the passage say?

2) What does it mean?

3) What does it mean for me?

---

1 <https://banneroftruth.org/us/resources/articles/2001/thomas-goodwin/>. Date accessed: 9th July, 2019.

Whether you read the Bible with the P.O.I.A. Method or another way, you can't get to application without thinking about God's Word. That's what disciples fundamentally do with God's Word—they think about it, carefully and deeply, which is to say they **meditate** on it.

By meditate, I don't mean disciples sit with their legs folded and hum. I'm not talking about thinking positively to shoo bad thoughts away, or emptying the mind as a Buddhist would. Rather, by meditate, I mean *filling* our minds with the truth of God's Word.

The Bible exhorts Christians to let God's Word dwell in us richly (Col. 3:16). What that means **is Christians should be full of the Bible**—it should be *on our minds* and *stored up in our hearts.* Charles Spurgeon, a famous preacher, once described a man who was so full of the Bible that, if he were cut, he would bleed Bible.

How do you become a Bible-bleeding disciple? **You meditate on God's Word.** You think about it day and night like the godly person in Psalm 1.

Many Christians get frustrated reading the Bible because they feel like they get nothing out of it, and on one level that's understandable. After all, sometimes the Bible is hard to understand; it's normal to not always get it—that's OK. Yet what these frustrated Christians don't realize is they may often get nothing out of what they read because they hardly spend any time *thinking* about what they've read. Thomas Watson put it like this: 'The reason we come away so cold from reading the Word is because we do not warm ourselves at the fires of meditation.'[2]

---

2 Thomas Watson, *Puritan Sermons* (reprint; Wheaton, IL: Richard Owens Roberts, 1981), v. 2, p. 62.

Yet if we will warm ourselves by this fire, if we will spend time thinking about God's Word, He promises that He will grant understanding (2 Tim. 2:7; Prov. 2:1-5). Understanding may come in small bits over time, but come it will. How then can we warm ourselves at the fire of meditation? Here are three suggestions:

1. **Read/Hear God's Word** — If we are going *to know God's Word, then we have to expose ourselves to it.* We can do this through what's often called a 'quiet time.' While this might sound like blanket time for babies, it's not. Rather, *a quiet time is a dedicated time Christians spend with God.* It's a time Jason spends alone with his heavenly Father—listening to Him through His Word and speaking to Him through prayer. One way to consistently have a quiet time is to set a regular time of the day, whenever it is, and stick to it day after day.

2. **Copy God's Word** — Another way to meditate on God's Word is simply to write it out word for word. This practice helps you to think about each word and, Lord willing, notice things you didn't notice before. Why not start with a short book, like Philippians, and copy a few verses during your quiet time?

3. **Memorize God's Word** — When he first came to Christ, Jason was especially helped by the verse that talked about God never leaving him (Heb. 13:5). So he spent a few days writing that verse out over and over again. By the tenth time, he had the verse memorized. All of a sudden, it was like the verse was always with him—on the train as he traveled across the city, at his job as he worked long days, on his mind when he was tempted to think horrible things about Al.

Maybe you hear these suggestions and think, 'I don't have a *quiet* time because I hardly have *any* time.' It's true—most people don't have a ton of time on their hands. Jason sure doesn't. Like you, he has responsibilities, plus the building he lives in is never all that quiet. Nonetheless, a quiet time can be had and enjoyed. Jason may simply have to crawl before he can run.

JASON

When he first began training through meditation, Jason crawled with a practice Eddy taught him called the **Three-Minute Exercise.** In this practice, Jason would

read the Bible (a verse or two) for a minute,

think about what he read for a minute,

and pray about what he read for a minute.

Again, **this is the starting line—not the finish line**—when it comes to spending time with God. After all, we won't usually *find* time in our schedules to add something, so we must *make* time. Yet we all need to start somewhere, and three-minute quiet time is much better than a zero-minute quiet time. So don't be discouraged if you need to begin your quiet times here. Be encouraged that you even want to have a quiet time.

'Jason, remember this point,' Eddy said, 'because too often Christians get caught up in how long their quiet times are.'

'They think a 20-minute quiet time should automatically produce a certain spiritual feeling or reward. If they skip or shrink this time, they feel like they can't approach God because they didn't show up for the morning drill, and now they're in some kind of spiritual timeout because God is mad at them. This thinking, however holy it might sound, is whack. It actually shows a reliance on our work to please God instead of Jesus' work. It forgets God took out His wrath on His Son for all who trust in Him, and He's not mad at us anymore!'

True, if we're not seeking God simply out of sheer laziness, we should repent. But every parent of little kids knows that some mornings seem to only start with new morning tantrums, not new morning mercies. In fact, rare are the days where a parent wakes up blissfully to serenity, gliding out of bed to a home as calm as a bubbling brook. And yet, it's at these points we should remember that while the Bible commands us to be still before God (Ps. 46:10), the Bible doesn't state how long or quiet our quiet times must be.

Rather, the Bible charges us to regularly think about, seek after, and yearn for Jesus (Heb. 12:1-2). Our duty is that simple, freeing, and delightful. When talking about meditation, we're not necessarily talking about sitting down in silence, however helpful that may be. We're talking more so about writing a verse on an index-card, putting it above your kitchen sink as you do the dishes and thinking about it. That's what it looks like to let the Word of God dwell in you richly.

'So don't put your hope in the length of your quiet time, brother Jason,' Eddy said.'Put it in the length of God's love. You're always abiding in Him anyway, and He has never left your side.'

Jason had no idea what Eddy meant about abiding in God, but he's finding the more he reads, copies, and memorizes, the more he's sharing in the experience described in Psalm 119:

I have stored up your word in my heart,
  that I might not sin against you.
Blessed are you, O Lord;
  teach me your statutes!
With my lips I declare
  all the rules of your mouth.
In the way of your testimonies I delight
  as much as in all riches.
(Ps. 119:11-14)

Where does meditation lead us? It leads us to prayer. Usually, when someone speaks to someone else, the other person responds. Bible reading and prayer are no different. Jason has heard from his heavenly Father through His Word. He's thought about what his Father has said. And now, he wants to respond to God, which leads us to a new part of his training—prayer.

MEMORY VERSE

'*I have stored up your word in my heart, that I might not sin against you*' (Ps. 119:11).

SUMMARY

We've learned how to read our Bibles through prayer, observation, interpretation, and application. As we take up reading the Bible, three rules help us to do so faithfully: 1) context, 2) context, 3) context. As we study the context of a passage and read and re-read it, we find ourselves meditating on Scripture, chewing on and savoring the meal of God's Word.

WHAT'S THE POINT?

Followers of Jesus pray like Jesus.

4. PRAYER: TALKING TO GOD

JASON

Al confused Jason. Now that Jason was following Jesus, Al would walk the other way whenever they saw each other. 'How did our relationship get like this?' Jason wondered.

After all, as kids, Al was the one who gave Jason advice about becoming a Christian. Jason remembered when he and Al were seven years old and sitting in the back seat of the city bus. At that time, Al called himself a Christian, and even seemed like one. So, as the bus rolled through the smog of their city streets, Jason asked his brother a question.

'Hey, how do I do that?'

'Do what?' Al asked.

'Be a Christian, like you. I want to be one. So, how do I do it?'

'Oh!' Al answered. 'Well, you have to pray.'

'Okay,' Jason said. The brothers sat silently for a few moments.

'For how long?' Jason asked. He didn't want to mess up this whole becoming-a-Christian-thing.

'Mmmm,' Al, the seven-year-old sage, hummed as he sat in thought. A few seconds passed, but they felt like a few hours. Jason waited on a deep answer. None came. Instead, Al shrugged his shoulders and responded.

'Like, five minutes,' he said.

'Ah, got it,' Jason said, now taking his turn to casually shrug his shoulders. Jason would never forget what he actually thought when he heard Al's answer.

'Five minutes? That's a long time to pray!'

This memory may be funny, but it also shows how people are confused about prayer. What is prayer? Why should Jesus' disciples pray? How do we know God hears our prayers? When should we pray, and how do we even do it? What should we pray for, and who should we pray to? In this chapter, we'll answer questions like these as Jason seeks to grow as one of Jesus' disciples.

WHAT IS PRAYER?

If the Bible is God talking to people, then *prayer is people*, specifically Christians, *talking to God*. 'Well, of course,' you might say. But consider this for a moment: The maker of the universe,

who created all things and

controls all things,

who raises the dead and

is full of goodness and love,

who offered His only Son to die in the place of sinners

this God invites His children to speak to Him at **any time**. Prayer is an incredible privilege.

Nonetheless, many Christians seem to take prayer for granted. Alistair Begg noted, '[Satan] has scored a great victory in getting sincere believers to waver in their conviction that prayer is necessary and powerful.'[1]

STOP:

If someone were to listen to your prayers this past week, would they think you believe prayer is necessary and powerful? Why or why not?

Maybe Satan has scored this victory by confusing people about *why* they should pray in the first place.

WHY SHOULD CHRISTIANS PRAY? HOW DO WE KNOW THAT GOD HEAR OUR PRAYERS?

Often Christians pray like they're talking to their genie instead of their God. They might not rub a lamp like Aladdin and wait for a mystical giant to pop out, but they ask for whatever they want, which isn't necessarily bad. God says, 'You do not have because you do not ask' (James 4:2, NIV). Jesus Himself commanded His followers to ask for whatever they wanted.

'Truly, truly, I say to you, whatever you ask of the Father in my name, he will give it to you.' (John 16:23)

But did Jesus mean that we should ask for whatever we want *for any reason we want?* Can Jason ask God for a million dollars to spend on himself and expect it in his bank account the next day?

Questions like these show the importance of training to read the Bible well. Remember what we learned in the last chapter: we want to be able to understand what God *says* and what He *means*. Some preacher might tell you that if you just pray with enough faith, you can get whatever you want and spend it on whoever you want, even yourself. But did Jesus *mean* that in John 16?

1 Alistair Begg, *Made For His Pleasure* (Chicago: Moody Press, 1996), p. 52.

He didn't. In fact, right after telling us that we don't have something because we don't pray for it, God clearly tells us that we still might not have what we prayed for because we prayed for it *with the wrong motives.*

'You ask and do not receive, because you ask wrongly, to spend it on your passions' (James 4:3)

Here, God means if we pray and don't get what we pray for, it may be because we're praying with sinful motives. So you pray to get a good grade on a test, but you really only want that grade so people think you're the best and brightest in the class; pride motivates your prayer. We need to remember God has scales that can weigh our motives (Prov. 16:2).

A declined prayer request doesn't always mean we've prayed with sinful motives, but it can. It's easy to think something is wrong with God when He doesn't grant our request, but **a declined prayer request ought to cause us to question *our* motives,** not God's. What's more, our sin is not the only reason God might not answer our prayers as we'd like. In Matthew 26:39, Jesus' request isn't granted, and He had no sin! In 2 Corinthians 12:8-9, God doesn't answer Paul's request as he hoped either. What's going on here? 1 John 5:14 lends some clarity:

'And this is the confidence that we have toward him, that if we ask anything ***according to his will*** *he hears us.'*

God won't grant us anything that goes against His will. We may not always know what His will is, but He has revealed all we need to know of it in the Bible. So if we're praying for something sinful, we know that's not God's will. Jason knows he *shouldn't* pray with selfish motivations, but why *should* he pray? The Bible provides a number of answers.

PRAYER GLORIFIES GOD

The Apostle Paul provided one main motivation for anything he did—he wanted to glorify God (1 Cor. 10:31). In other words, he wanted to honor God and show that he is worthy of all honor. So,

when Christians pray to God,

praising Him for who He is and what He's done,

He's glorified.

When we're honest about who we are,

confessing our sins to Him in prayer,

He's glorified.

When we thank Him for something or someone,

recognizing He's the giver of all good gifts,

He's glorified.

When we ask Him for something,

realizing that our problems are greater than our resources and

trusting that God is able to answer,

He's glorified.

Jesus said, 'Whatever you ask in my name, this I will do, that the Father may be glorified in the Son' (John 14:13). He is happy to answer our prayers so our Father may be glorified!

Christians want to glorify God, *and prayer glorifies God.* So, Christians want to pray.

PRAYER EXPRESSES FAITH

Prayer is the language of faith; prayer is putting faith on our lips. It's one of the most basic ways Christians express their trust in God. Whenever Christians pray, we're saying, 'God, I trust you are who you say you are.' We may not trust Him as much as we should, but it's not the amount of our trust that matters when we pray; it's *who we're trusting in* that matters. That's why Jesus said we could have faith the size of a mustard seed, which is about 1-2 millimeters, and we would be able to throw a mountain into the sea (Luke 17:6). When we pray, we're showing who we ultimately trust in—God. He commands us to pray (1 Thess. 5:17). Our prayers show we trust His command is good, and so Christians want to pray.

It's the object, not the size, of our faith that matters.

PRAYER DEFENDS FAITH

The Christian life is a battle against our sin, the Devil, and a sinful world. God gives us weapons for that battle and describes them in passages like Ephesians 6:17-18:

'Take the helmet of salvation, and the sword of the Spirit, which is the word of God, ***praying at all times in the Spirit, with all prayer and supplication.*** *To that end, keep alert with all perseverance, making supplication for all the saints…'*

God calls Christians to pray continuously. This doesn't mean we need to be verbally praying every second of the day, but it does mean that *prayer is to be a normal part of a Christian's life*. Too often, we only pray when we're in a crisis. Of course, we should pray in these moments, but Christians ought to pray regularly, not just on an as-needed basis. If we only pray to God when we feel like we need Him, our faith will be weak and more open to attacks from Satan. What's more, we'll lose sight of the truth **that we always need God; it's just sometimes we feel our need**.

But if we pray regularly, we'll strengthen our faith because we'll have defended it using this weapon. At first, the weapon of prayer may seem weak, ordinary, and foolish, but God's kingdom isn't of this world—and neither are His weapons (2 Cor. 10:4). When we pray, we're not only expressing our faith in that fact, we're defending that faith. And so Christians want to pray.

PRAYER SERVES OTHERS

Did you catch the last part of the verse from Ephesians 6? Paul commands Christians to continue praying for *all* the saints. Praying for ourselves is a good thing, but we shouldn't *rob ourselves of the joy of also praying for others*. God has given us prayer so we could love our neighbors. So pray for them as you'd like to be prayed for.

If someone looked at your prayer life, would they see someone attentive to the concerns of others? Or does your prayer life reflect that you only care about you? When is the last time you prayed for your pastor? If the Apostle Paul knew he needed prayer and asked for it (Eph. 6:19-20), your pastor does, too.

Or has someone in your life ever gotten on your nerves? Instead of complaining about them, pray for them! Prayer has a unique power to help our affections for others. The Bible urges Christians to pray for one another, and so Christians want to pray for one another.

GOD HEARS PRAYER

Finally, we ought to pray because God hears our prayers. We know He does because He says He does, if we ask as He's told us to in His Word. We've seen that God's Word says we shouldn't pray for sinful reasons. It also tells us we should pray in Jesus' name (John 16:23). To pray in Jesus' name is to come to God based on what Jesus has done, not what we've done. It's to pray believing our Father is pleased with Jesus, and we can only come to Him through Jesus. It's to pray boldly with the authority of the one who has been given all authority (Matt. 28:18). To pray in Jesus' name is to affirm that

Jesus is the way,

the truth, and

the life (John 14:6),

and that we trust in His promises.

The point isn't that we robotically say the words 'In Jesus' name' at the end of our prayers, as if that phrase is a kind of heavenly hall pass for our prayers. Our hope isn't that God hears our prayers because we say the right words; our hope is that **God hears our prayers because of Jesus**. Sometimes, Christians want a big sign to prove God is there and that He listens. But we have something better than a sign; we have a Savior.

Where we've failed to obey God's commands, like the command to pray, Jesus succeeded. Jesus prayed perfectly, and because of His sinless life, death, and resurrection—and our trust in it—we're now free to come to God boldly and pray as our Savior did. *Jesus has done everything required so we can stand righteous before God*. A benefit of being among the righteous is having your prayers heard by God. 'The Lord is far from the wicked,' the Bible says, 'but he hears the prayer of the righteous' (Prov. 15:29).

God not only hears our prayers; *He delights in them* (Prov. 15:8). Like good parents who delight in hearing from their kids, *God is happy to hear from us*. Even though our prayers may be weak, our Savior is strong.

Earlier, we asked why we should pray, but looking at these five reasons, the better question is why *wouldn't* we pray? We have the opportunity to glorify God, trust Him, defend our faith, serve others, and be heard by our heavenly Father. He invites us to pray because He cares for us:

'Therefore humble yourselves under the mighty hand of God, that He may exalt you in due time, casting all your care upon Him, ***for He cares for you.'*** (1 Pet. 5:6–7, CSB)

It's been said that worrying—or over-thinking—is often a sign of under-praying.[2] Prayer is one basic way for Christians enjoy the care and peace of God (Phil. 4:4-7). And so Christians want to pray!

STOP:

Do any of these reasons surprise you? Why or why not?

WHEN & HOW DO I PRAY?

Ephesians 6 also showed us how often we should pray—we're to pray 'at all times' (Eph. 6:18). So, what does praying 'at all times' look like? Jesus shows us, but we have to look at His example carefully. Why?

Because it's easy to look at Jesus and think we ought to do everything He does. But *Jesus isn't simply our perfect model for how to do things;* **He's also our perfect Savior from the wrong things we've done.** Remember, Jesus has done what we can't. He's the hero of the story. So if we're going to look to Him as a model, then we should remember it's not our job to be the hero; it's our job to *trust* the hero. Before we see how we can obey the command to pray, we should see how Jesus has already done so. Seeing Jesus' perfect obedience frees us from obeying God in our own strength.

---

2 James Roberson, <https://twitter.com/jtrob3/status/1029678765398523904>. Date accessed: 5th July 2019.

It keeps us grateful and focused on the hero of our faith, who gives us strength to be like Him in the right ways.

Looking at Jesus' life, we see **He prayed at all times.**

He prayed before He performed miracles (Matt. 14:19);

He left big crowds and went to pray in quiet places (Luke 5:16);

He prayed when he had big problems (Luke 22:41-42).

Know that God can handle all of our issues at any time.

ILLUSTRATION

If you came into my bedroom to ask me something at 3 a.m., that would be creepy, and I'd probably call the police. However, if my young daughter came into my room to ask me something at 3 a.m., while I might not love the time she chose, I would understand why she chose to come. The difference between you and my daughter is that she has access to me, she has the right to me. Timothy Keller wrote, '*The only person who dares wake up a king at 3 a.m. for a glass of water is a child. We have that kind of access.*'[3]

As sons and daughters of God, we have this kind of access to our Heavenly Father. Even better, God never gets annoyed with us; He's not like a neighbor we bother early in the morning (Prov. 27:14). God needs no sleep, and so, like Jesus, we can come to Him at any time.

But Jesus not only modeled *when* to pray, He also modeled *how* to pray.

---

3 Timothy Keller, <https://twitter.com/timkellernyc/status/569890726349307904?lang=en> Date Accessed: 7th August 2019.

Earlier, we considered how prayer defended faith. In Ephesians 6:18, Paul not only told Christians when to pray ('at all times') but how to pray—'in the Spirit.' Only Christians have God's Spirit in them (Rom. 8:9, 14). All who have the Spirit are sons and daughters of God. Why does this truth matter when we're considering how Jesus modeled prayer? It matters because Jesus instructed God's sons and daughters to pray to their heavenly Father. If we're not a son or daughter, if we're not in the family, then we can't pray to the Father.

When to pray: At all times (Eph. 6:18; 1 Thess. 5:17)

How to pray: In the Spirit

'Our Father.' Those are the first two words of the prayer Jesus models. In Matthew 6:9-13, Jesus showed us how to pray:

'Pray then like this:

"Our Father in heaven,
hallowed be your name.
Your kingdom come,
your will be done,
on earth as it is in heaven.
Give us this day our daily bread,
and forgive us our debts,
as we also have forgiven our debtors.
And lead us not into temptation,
but deliver us from evil."'

Now, Jesus didn't command us to pray only this prayer, though it's a wonderful one to pray. He commanded us to pray *like* this prayer. How do we do that?

We pray to our Father in heaven (v. 9)

Prayer reflects the unity we have with all other Christians. We all pray to the same Father because we're all members of the same family. The prayer Jesus gives us reminds us that prayer isn't just for you, but for *us, so we pray to* ***our*** *Father.* What's more, prayer reminds us that the kingdom of this world isn't ultimately our home; the kingdom of heaven is where we belong, and God rules the universe from there. And so Christians pray to their Father in heaven.

We ask His will to be done (v. 10)

The more we grow as Christians, the more we want God's kingdom and purpose to expand, not our own. The more we grow as Christians, the more we want to pray that God's will is done, not our own. That's what Jesus did. 'Your will be done' is what Jesus prayed in what was perhaps His most stressful moment on earth (Luke 22:42). Our prayers ought to echo His. And so Christians pray for their Father's will to be done.

We ask Him to provide what we need (v. 11)

Jesus teaches us to ask for our daily bread. He talks about bread because that's what God gave His people every day when He rescued them from Egypt (Exod 16). Sending them bread from heaven, God took care of His people. He showed them He is God, and they should trust Him. Likewise, prayer expresses our trust in God. When we go to God and ask Him for our daily needs,

we show that we recognize all good gifts come from Him,

and we give ourselves another opportunity to thank Him for those gifts. (James 1:17)

One wonderful detail about Jesus' prayer is that it's not long. When we pray, we often wonder why we're saying the words we're saying. But we don't have to convince God with many words. The context of Matthew 6 shows us this truth. Right before His model prayer, Jesus reminds us that God knows what we need anyway (Matt. 6:8). And so Christians can pray simple prayers, asking their Father who knows all and provides for all His children's physical needs.

We ask Him to provide what we *most* need (v. 11)

Look again at verse 11. Jesus not only teaches us to pray for our physical needs but also our deepest spiritual need, *the forgiveness of our sins.*

The only way to meet this need is through Jesus;

He's the only way for our sins to be forgiven. He's the only way to spiritual life,

and that's exactly what the bread from heaven was meant to show God's people (John 6:35).

Remember in Chapter One how we talked about the need to confess our sins? Here, Jesus models that for us, not because He had any sins to confess, but because the people He was teaching did. **A Christian who knows their sins have been forgiven through Jesus will naturally forgive others**, not because our forgiving others is the way to be accepted by God, but because it is *proof that we've already been accepted by Him.*

In short, **forgiven people forgive people**. What's more, forgiven people admit they need help. The prayer Jesus modeled isn't a prayer for spiritual superheroes; it's a prayer for spiritual wimps. It's a prayer that can only be prayed if we know we need deliverance from evil. *Christians need forgiveness and protection from evil, and so we pray for our Father to provide our spiritual needs.*

Isn't it so kind of Jesus to model how God's children ought to pray? If we have the Spirit, then we can pray to the Father. What's even better—the Spirit helps us pray! The Bible gives us this promise:

'Likewise the Spirit helps us in our weakness. For we do not know what to pray for as we ought, but the Spirit himself intercedes for us with groanings too deep for words.' (Rom. 8:26)

If you're unsure how to pray, that's OK. God says that's to be expected. That's why this chapter is about basic, biblical instruction on prayer.

So, how do Christians pray?

We pray in the Spirit,

through the Son,

and to the Father.

When we know how to pray, we don't have to worry about whether or not we're 'doing it right.' When we know how to pray, we can enjoy freedom.

We can pray out loud or in our head.

We can pray short prayers and long prayers.

We can pray on our knees or standing up.

We can pray using our own words,

or using God's Word.

One wonderful habit to develop is to *pray the Bible back to God*. Why not take what you read in your quiet time and turn it into what you pray? As Don Whitney noted, 'Christian people—often do not pray simply because they do not feel like it. And the reason they don't feel like praying is that when they do pray, they tend to say the same old things about the same old things.'[4] Praying

4 Donald S. Whitney, *Praying the Bible* (Wheaton, IL: Crossway, 2015), p. 11.

the Bible gives our prayers fresh words for what may seem like routine topics.

JASON

Sometimes, Jason thinks he knows what he wants most in life, and he asks God for it. But he's starting to be glad God hasn't given him everything he thought he wanted. He's learning God's 'no' is better than His 'yes'.

What's more, Jason is learning that even though God doesn't give him everything he wants, God gives him everything he needs. What he most needed in life was a perfect record before God and a clean heart that comes with it. After sinning, David prayed to God, asking Him to create in him a clean heart (Ps. 51). Jason is starting to pray Psalm 51; he's starting to pray God's Word back to Him. What he's seeing is a new heart is leading him to live a new kind of life. It's leading him to worship—the final topic to consider for Jason's personal training.

MEMORY VERSE

'Likewise, the Spirit helps us in our weakness. For we do not know what to pray for as we ought, but the Spirit himself intercedes for us with groanings too deep for words' (Rom. 8:26).

SUMMARY

In this chapter, we learned that prayer is Christians talking to God. Prayer is a great responsibility, opportunity, and privilege. We should pray because it glorifies God, expresses our faith, defends our faith, and serves others. We should pray because God hears us and cares for us, and we can pray because of Jesus, who gives us access to God, and who models when and how to pray.

WHAT'S THE POINT?

Followers of Jesus worship God with their entire lives.

5. WORSHIP: LIVING FOR GOD

JASON

'What do you think it means to worship God, Jason?' Eddy asked.

'Uh, well, when I was a kid I thought worship were the couple of songs my mom sang before some preacher got up and talked for too long. I like the songs now, most of them, at least.'

As Jason trains for godliness, he's learning worship is more than singing. He's learning that in response to God's mercy, he should give his entire self to God, as God calls all Christians to do. *God has made every part of us,* **and paid for our every sin**. We were bought with a price (see 1 Cor. 6:19-20). We owe everything to God, so we don't just offer a portion of ourselves to Him. Rather, we give Him our all. This truth matters because it helps Jason think well about worship.

STOP:

How would you define worship, and why would you define it that way?

WHAT IS WORSHIP?

As we said in Chapter 1, we're not just trying to think about spiritual disciplines, we're trying to think *biblically* about them. So how does the Bible define worship? Romans and Hebrews help us:

 *'I appeal to you therefore, brothers, by the mercies of God, to present your bodies as a living sacrifice, holy and acceptable to God,* ***which is your spiritual worship****.'* (Rom. 12:1)

 *'Therefore let us be grateful for receiving a kingdom that cannot be shaken, and thus let us* ***offer to God acceptable worship****, with reverence and awe.'* (Heb. 12:28)

What is worship according to the Bible? Most basically, **worship is a Christian's right response to God.**

'Worship is the proper response of the creature to the Creator,' says D.A. Carson.[1] *It's offering ourselves to God.* When we understand the gospel and what it means for our lives, we want to give all of ourselves to God.[2] In short, while songs are wonderful and a part of worship, worship is much more than a song. As Matt Boswell put it, '"Worship" is too heavy a doctrine for "singing" to bear by itself.'[3] Indeed a local church worships God as it meets, what's often called 'corporate worship'—we'll talk more about this in the next chapter. Yet worship is more than a church meeting.

While our definition of worship may be short, it's not shallow. Romans 12:1 and Hebrews 12:28 provide at least four ways to think about offering ourselves to God. Our worship is:

1) *God-focused*
2) *total*
3) *fearful*
4) *grateful*

---

1 D.A. Carson, *Worship by the Book* (Grand Rapids, MI: Zondervan, 2002), p. 29.

2 David Peterson, *Engaging with God* (Downers Grove, Il: IVP, 1992), p. 242.

3 Matt Boswell, <https://twitter.com/MattBoswell/status/1015765557784776706?s=20>. Date accessed: 5th July 2019.

JASON

When Jason first heard this definition, he found it really strict. After all, isn't worship about how we express ourselves and connect with God? But after giving it some thought, he found this definition freeing, and I hope you will too.

WORSHIP IS GOD-FOCUSED

Worship is about God. Like all things, *it's for God,* and *it begins with God* (Rom. 11:36). This is why we defined worship as a right *response* to God—*it begins with Him, not us.* So Christians respond to who God is and what He's done. What's more, God is so gracious to draw us to respond to Him.

In both Romans 12 and Hebrews 12, we see that worship is directed toward God and no one else. This matters because as sinful people, we want to worship ourselves, not God.

JASON

'Decades ago, when I went to university,' Eddy said to Jason, 'I thought I knew what it meant to live a godly life. I lived like I was all grown up spiritually and could handle things on my own, but I quickly fell into a life of sin, of partying, of all the world says university should be. I didn't live a life of worship to God; I lived a life that worshipped me.'

All people worship something. The question is *who or what* do you worship? That's why we're talking about a *right* kind of worship. If you read Genesis 1, you'll see that *people were made to worship God.* But after sin entered the picture in Genesis 3, people didn't hunger to worship their God, they hungered to worship their selves. At the Tower of Babel, people didn't want to worship God's name; they wanted to worship their own name (Gen. 11:4). Right worship, however, is about God, and so Christians worship God alone:

'You shall have no other gods before me. You shall not make for yourself an image in the form of anything in heaven above or on the earth beneath or in the waters below. You shall not bow down to them or ***worship*** *them.'* (Exod. 20:3-5, NIV)

Some translations of the Bible use the word 'serve' instead of 'worship.' That's because *worship is service*, and what the Bible makes clear is that *our service is ultimately to be to God.* **As Christians, we no longer serve ourselves; we offer ourselves to God.** The greatest commandment makes this point:

'You shall love the Lord your God with all your heart and with all your soul and with all your mind and with all your strength.' (Mark 12:30)

We're to love God first and foremost, and we're to love Him with our all—our total selves.

WORSHIP IS TOTAL

Remember the P.O.I.A. Method from Chapter 2? It's so helpful on this point. Take a few moments now to **pray** that God would help you understand Mark 12:30.

Next, let's **observe.** Re-read Mark 12:30, and ask yourself, 'which words are repeated?' *Circle those words every time they appear.* The word we'll focus on is the word 'all.' You should have at least four circles because four times, God calls us to love Him with our all.

Now, let's **interpret** by looking at the broader context of Mark 12:30. In Mark 12:29, a teacher asks Jesus which commandment is the most important. Look closely at Jesus' answer:

Jesus answered, *'The most important is, "Hear, O Israel: The Lord our God, the Lord is one."'*

Why does Jesus talk about God being one right before He talks about how we love God with our all? One Bible teacher said it's because God is teaching us that *God is undivided.*

And because God is like that, then He must be approached and worshiped by an undivided person: all your heart, all your soul, all your strength. In other words, all of you. Every single bit. God is not pulled in different directions. So neither should we be in our worship of Him. Real faith and trust in God are not compartmentalized. God is not looking for people who can give Him their strength—mending the church roof or serving in short-term missions—while their greatest loves and deepest desires are directed elsewhere.[4]

So Mark 12:29-30 means we should love God with our all; our worship should be undivided; it should be total.

Now let's **apply** this truth.

JASON

In short, for Jason it means he can't worship God on Sunday and keep getting drunk with Al on Friday. It means on Thursday afternoon, when Jason is at work, he should be honest in his dealings. As a Christian, Jason advertises what God is like, and if Jason is a cheat, he teaches people God is a cheat! God didn't save Jason so he could just sing a song or two Sunday morning; he saved Jason for Monday night, Wednesday afternoon, and Friday night. All of Jason is God's all the time, and the good news is because of Jesus—all of God is Jason's all the time.

The Scriptures say: 'Come, let us worship and bow down; let us kneel before the Lord, our Maker!' (Psalm 95:6, CSB). Worship is about recognizing what God is worth and responding accordingly.

4 David Gibson, *Living Life Backward* (Wheaton, Il: Crossway, 2017), p. 80.

We might respond through song.

We might respond through reading God's Word and prayer.

This kind of worship is directly to God, and *if we're not thinking about God while we sing, pray, or read—we're not really worshiping.*[5] Jesus talked about people who honoured Him with their lips, but their hearts were far from Him (Matt. 15:8).

And yet, there is a kind of worship that we offer indirectly to God, too. Direct worship is the what we do as we think about God—things like singing, praying, reading the Bible. But doing the dishes or driving your car are worship to God as well. We don't have to be thinking about God as we drive for it to be worship: '*O God, I praise you as I make this left turn!*' Rather, if we're doing it as He says to—which in this example means we're driving lawfully—we're indirectly praising Him. All of our life then—whether indirectly or directly—can point to God, and so all of our life can be worship.[6] To sum it up:

- How we **think** is for God (Phil. 3:19-20; 4:8).
- How we **speak** is for God (Eph. 4:29).
- How we **spend our money** and **enjoy God's gifts** is for God (1 Timothy 6:17).
- How we **work** is for God (Col. 3:23-24).
- How we **eat and drink—*whatever we do, all we do***—should be for God (1 Cor. 10:31).

---

5 Donald S. Whitney, *Spiritual Disciplines for the Christian Life* (Colorado Springs, CO: NavPress, 2014), p. 106.

6 I'm indebted to Matt Merker for the categories of direct and indirect worship.

WORSHIP IS FEARFUL

Total worship helps us to think about fearful worship. Why? Hebrews 12:28 helps us. Remember how it spoke about worshiping God with reverence and awe. Those are words we don't often use. What do they mean? They mean to live in the fear of God.

The 'fear of the Lord' is a phrase you'll run into the more you read the Bible. When we look at the Bible and what it says about fearing God, we see that to fear God means to be in awe of God. When we fear God, we see how clean from dirtiness He is, how far from evil He is—and we tremble accordingly. This is our basic job description—to fear God, our judge (Eccles. 12:13).

Maybe the fear of God is better depicted than defined. In the Bible, a man named Isaiah sees a glimpse of God, and he shows us what the fear of God looks like.

'*In the year that King Uzziah died, I saw the Lord, high and exalted, seated on a throne; and the train of his robe filled the temple. Above him were seraphim, each with six wings: With two wings they covered their faces, with two they covered their feet, and with two they were flying. And they were calling to one another:*

"Holy, holy, holy is the Lord Almighty;
the whole earth is full of his glory."

At the sound of their voices the doorposts and thresholds shook and the temple was filled with smoke.

"Woe to me!" I cried. "I am ruined! For I am a man of unclean lips, and I live among a people of unclean lips, and my eyes have seen the King, the Lord Almighty."' (Isa. 6:1-5, NIV)

Fear of the Lord includes hatred of evil (Prov. 8:13). When Isaiah sees God for how holy He is—how different He is than everything else—he responds by hating his sin, his evil. If you keep reading the passage, you'll see that Isaiah, after having his sins paid for, wants to obey God and serve Him with his entire life (vv. 6-8).

Isaiah's example shows us that to fear God means to serve Him with your whole life because you know God is the ruler, judge, and savior of your life.

> **And so we serve him reverently, which means showing Him appropriate respect.**

Yet that respect doesn't just look like sitting up straight during church. Rather, reverent worship is to serve the holy God and respond to Him according to His Word. In His Word, God has laid out the terms for how we should serve Him, which is why we defined worship as a *right* response to God. As Vaughan Roberts said, 'There is such a thing as false worship that does not please God.'[7] And so Christians worship God reverently, which is to say they worship him rightly, even fearfully.

WORSHIP IS GRATEFUL

And yet, worship isn't only about having the appropriate respect, but also taking the appropriate delight in God and His gifts (Deut. 28:47; 1 Tim. 6:17). We ought to enjoy God and what He's given us, and we ought to do so with grateful hearts.

We can't miss this point: *Right worship is grateful worship*. Guilt and shame shouldn't motivate us. We should never live for God because we feel like we have to, since, you know, God said so and He bought us with His Son's blood. Worship is not a transaction!

---

7 Vaughan Roberts, *True Worship* (Milton Keynes: Authentic, 2002), Kindle edition, Introduction. See also David Peterson's *Engaging with God*: 'From a biblical point of view, the worship of the living and true God is essentially an engagement with him on the terms that he proposes and in the way that he alone makes possible' (p. 55).

Rather, *joy should motivate our worship*—joy that comes from knowing **Jesus has freed us from guilt and shame**; joy that comes from receiving good gifts from a gracious Father. What ought to motivate our worship is the fact that we even *get to* worship the one true God. A Christian growing in godliness will see worship less as a job and more as a joy.

STOP:

Do you see worship as a joy? Is worship just a routine that you do before the preacher preaches, or is it what we've described in this chapter?

Look back at Hebrews 12:28. The author gives one reason to gratefully praise God: as Christians, we've received God's Kingdom. We're citizens of it (Phil. 3:20). Though we were unworthy, *God has given us this incredible gift, and the price He paid was the priceless blood of His own Son.* To worship only out of a sense of duty is to miss the beauty of the gospel. Gratitude is the language of heaven—everyone there expresses thanks, yet no one speaks this dialect in hell.

So true worship is service motivated by gratitude for the gospel and the hope it gives to us. That's why Christians worship God gratefully.

We've seen that true worship is *a right response to God*. It's service that

starts with God,

is focused on God, and

without God's work *in* our lives,

we could not worship God *with* our lives.

Christian worship is fearful, and yet, as we just rejoiced in—*Christian worship is grateful.* Christians are people who grow to see two things more clearly. On one hand, they see what they deserve. On the other hand, they see how kindly God has treated them in Christ.

And so Christians worship.

JASON

Why does this all matter for Jason? Thinking rightly about worship will help free him from worshiping wrongly.

> ***It frees him** from thinking that the only real way he can connect with God is through music he likes.*
>
> ***It frees him** from thinking that worship must include an emotional, spiritual high 'as if worship was something you snorted through your nose.'*[8]

Jason used to think that super spiritual worship happened when people lifted their arms during the music at church. There's nothing wrong with doing that; the author of this book does it from time to time. But the truths we've looked at remind us that *worship is more about honoring God with our lives, not just our arms.*

> Furthermore, these truths free Jason from living as if the world revolves around him.

People who aren't Christians want to worship me, myself, and I. But Christians want to worship the

> Father,
>
> Son,
>
> and Spirit.

---

8 Roberts, *True Worship,* ch. 2.

While singing God's praises is bringing Jason more joy, he's also finding joy in encouraging other Christians and hearing *them* sing God's praises. As we think about Jason's training, we're going to turn to his public training. We're going to look at the things Christians do with other people, and why Jason ought to join in those activities if he's truly training for godliness. We're going to begin with a group of people you might not expect—a church.

MEMORY VERSE

'You shall love the Lord your God with all your heart and with all your soul and with all your mind and with all your strength' (Mark 12:30).

SUMMARY

In this chapter, we learned that worship is a Christian's right response to God. According to the Bible, our worship is God-focused, total, fearful, and grateful. Worship can be individual, as we've talked about in this chapter, or corporate, as we'll talk about in the next. Though we may worship God directly or indirectly, all of our lives should point to Him. That's what we were made for, and that's what Jesus paid for.

WHAT'S THE POINT?

Followers of Jesus don't follow Jesus alone.

6. CHURCH: LOVING YOUR FAMILY

JASON

It's Sunday morning, and Jason walks in and sees Ms. Pearl. She has loved Jesus twice as long as Jason has been alive. She's wearing her classic velvet jumpsuit—burgundy—and silver hair sits braided on her head like a crown. Her sneakers, puffy and white, look like clouds. Though they seem soft, the Velcro straps are sealed tight. Ms. Pearl is old. Ms. Pearl is an African-American from the Southern United States. And Ms. Pearl is here to praise God and to encourage her brothers and sisters in Christ.

She can't stand up to sing given her hip problems, but she's there, in the same room as Jason—a young man of Irish descent. Sitting in her usual seat in the second row, Ms. Pearl waves over at Marie, Jason's mother, inviting her to sit with her. Marie honored the invitation, and Jason figured he would, too. Jason didn't understand the spiritual things Ms. Pearl said all that well, but when he looked up, he saw her hugging his mother tightly. Not letting go, she began passionately praying for her.

This seemed like a private affair, so Jason, feeling a little awkward, looked across the room at something else. He was relieved to spot Eddy. A decade ago, a judge released Eddy from prison. Eddy still struggled to land a good job given his record, but that hasn't stopped him from buying Jason food when they meet up. Though he has little money, Eddy has lots of love. He'd usually stop and talk with Jason, but he was busy setting up chairs for folks coming into the room. He had a few volunteers to help him, but he was still sweating. Jason remembered that Eddy was a deacon, whatever that meant.

More people piled into the room. Patrick, a rich Filipino man, came and sat in the front row next to Zamari, a graduate student home on break. Patrick's wife died from cancer last year, and Zamari just got engaged. Patrick asked Zamari how her proposal went down, and he seemed so happy for her Jason thought it was *Patrick* who got engaged.

The Johnsons, a family of, well, a lot, stumbled into the room next. They're a bit late and a bit loud, despite their best attempt to sneak in undetected. Mr. Johnson was holding his one-year-old daughter, Chloe, like a football. Pregnant Mrs. Johnson kept apologizing to people since Chloe was throwing her Cheerios at people. Folks just laughed. Looking for seats, Mr. and Mrs. Johnson looked like they were holding on to their sanity as much as they were holding on to their kids. But the Johnsons were there and seemed eager to be so.

In the front corner of the room, a Brazilian sister sits behind a piano. A Korean brother sits on top of a cajón. Both wait to start playing, as a pastor stands up at the front of the room.

'Good morning, beloved,' he greets everyone. His warm words feel like a verbal hug. 'God has given us grace to gather once again.'

'HALLELUJAH—YES HE DID!' Ms. Pearl shouts, rocking back and forth in her seat with a crooked smile and one hand raised. Her other hand grips her cane.

Zamari's eyes opened wide after Ms. Pearl's outbreak. It had been a while since Zamari visited this place, but she found out what everyone else seemed to know: with each passing month, dear Ms.

Pearl got more lively. She leaned over to Jason, and said with a smile: 'God is too good, baby, and I ain't gon' let the rocks cry out for me.'

Jason had no idea what she meant, and yet, the pastor up front kept smiling and kept speaking. As he did, Jason listened.

What is this place? What is this place where rich and poor, old and young, black and white gather together and serve one another?

It's a church.

PUBLIC TRAINING

In the first half of this book, we looked at personal training—spiritual disciplines Christians do individually as they follow Jesus. We thought about the disciplines of:

Bible reading,

prayer,

and worship.

Now, as *we turn to public training,* we're thinking about spiritual disciplines Christians do with others. In this chapter, we'll look at ways Christians love other Christians. In the next chapter, we'll see how Christians can love people who aren't Christians.

In the last chapter, Jason learned that **the Christian life isn't just the Sunday life, but everyday life.** And yet, that doesn't mean what happens on Sundays is unimportant. In fact, the Bible has a lot to say about church. In the first place it teaches us what church is.

STOP:

When you hear the word 'church,' what comes to mind? Who comes to mind?

WHAT IS CHURCH?

The Bible talks about the church in two basic ways. First, there's what's called the *universal* church. *The universal church is all Christians from all times from all over the world.* The Bible talks about the universal church in verses like Colossians 1:28:

> '[Jesus] is the head of the body.'

This image of the church as a body is important because we can't know *what the church is* without knowing *whose it is,* and Colossians 1 clarifies that the church belongs to Jesus. If Jason is in the body, he's connected to the head.

Jason gets to rejoice in the fact he's connected to Jesus, but that also means something special for his relationships with other Christians—namely, he's also connected to them. *All Christians are different parts of the same body, so we're all connected to one another.*

We're brothers and sisters Jesus died to rescue and bring to the Father.

We're brothers and sisters who all have the same Spirit, the Holy Spirit (Eph. 4:3).

When Jesus gathers the universal church, it'll be made up of people from all over the world (Rev. 7:9). Christians are deeply connected to one another because we're connected to Jesus.

JASON

This means Jason has more in common with Ms. Pearl, his sister who Jesus bought with His blood, than he does with Al, his brother by blood.

The universal church is an incredible thing. Yet there's another way the Bible talks about the church; *it talks about what's commonly called the local church.*

The Bible talks about the universal Church and the local church.

Paul wrote to specific churches in specific cities (1 Thess. 1:1), and he also wrote to multiple local churches in an area (Gal. 1:2).

A local church is a gathering of Christians who meet regularly in one place to hear God's Word taught and to celebrate baptism and the Lord's Supper. I'll explain this definition as we keep going, but for now let's break down one basic thing. *When the Bible talks about the local church, it means an assembly of people.* This means that a local church is not a place—it's a group of people. To have a church, you don't need a building with a steeple; you need the people of God, Christians. Those Christians can meet outside, or in a hotel, a favela, or a compound—wherever. The point is that *they meet regularly and are committed to God's Word and to each other.*

The local church is where parts of the invisible church gather and become visible. It's where the family of God gathers.

In Mark 10:29-30, Jesus promises that any Christian who would leave their home for His sake would find family:

Jesus said, 'Truly, I say to you, there is no one who has left house or brothers or sisters or mother or father or children or lands, for my sake and for the gospel, who will not receive a hundredfold now in this time, houses and brothers and sisters and mothers and children and lands.'

Where is it that Christians can find brothers, sisters, and mothers? In the church. With all this family language, it's no wonder why Paul would call the church 'the household of faith' (Gal. 6:10). Just as our biological families make up households, our spiritual families do, too.

STOP:

Have you experienced family life at church? If so, what was that like? If not, what would you want that to be like, and what do you think God would want it to be like?

Paul writes a lot about how the household of faith should be set up, and a part of that set up includes two things every church should have: elders and deacons.

> **In the Bible, *we find that every church should have elders* (Titus 1:5; Acts 14:23).**

ILLUSTRATION

One common picture of Christians is that we're sheep. If Jesus is the Chief Shepherd of the sheep as 1 Peter 5 says, then *elders are junior shepherds or under-shepherds.* **Elders are shepherds who** *protect the sheep God has given them. They oversee what is going on in the church, and make sure that the congregation is being taught truth from God's Word, not lies from God's enemy.*

> **Deacons are people like Eddy who serve the church by doing administrative tasks so that the church won't be divided.**

ILLUSTRATION

Think of deacons like waiters at a restaurant. They serve so that others can come and enjoy themselves, not fight over food. Acts 6 gives us an example of this kind of fighting in the local church, and it seems deacons are the solution.

Who should be an elder or a deacon? Paul lists the qualifications for these roles in 1 Timothy 3, but a short answer is that *godly men who are able to teach can serve as elders, and godly men and women can serve as deacons.*

Jason is seeing that the Bible has a lot to say about church—what it is, whose it is, and how it's structured. He can't always keep it straight, but he's learned enough to know that **God cares a lot about the local church.**

So, we know a little bit about what a local church is. But what actually happens when the family of God gathers?

WHAT HAPPENS AT CHURCH?

Church is the weekly family reunion for God's people, and here are five main things that take place when they gather.

1. At church, God's Word is preached. (Acts 2:41-42) In Acts 2, we find the beginning of the local church.[1] Peter preaches one of the first Christian sermons (2:14-41). And how do people respond?

So those who received [Peter's] word were baptized, and there were added that day about three thousand souls. And they devoted themselves to the apostles' teaching and the fellowship, to the breaking of bread and the prayers.

A love for God's Word marked the early church. They devoted themselves to its teaching. If disciples are students, as we said in Chapter One, then the local church is a school. And it has everything you'd expect a good school to have:

teachers,

discipline,

correction,

instruction.

---

1 I'm indebted to Capitol Hill Baptist Church's 'Life Together' Membership class for this point and the next one.

God's people gather around God's Word. It's the campfire the family gathers around during its weekly reunions.

So, when you go to church—put your ears to work. Listen carefully to God's Word as it's taught. *Go to church to be equipped, not entertained.* Don't sit there and just criticize the teaching; *sit under God's Word as one who needs it, not as one who judges it.*

Someone once asked a pastor why he preaches the gospel week after week, and he responded, 'Because you forget it week after week.' When asked by a church member why he preaches so long, another pastor responded 'Because you sin so long!' Though funny, these pastors' responses capture our need to hear God's Word every week.

2. At church, God's Word is believed, and believers are baptized. (Acts 2:41-42) Did you see what else happened when God's Word went out in Acts 2? People believed it! Faith came through hearing, as Romans 10 says. Verse 41 makes clear that people 'received' the Word for what it was—the truth. And they responded by being baptized, just as Jesus commanded disciples to do in Matthew 28:19.

Baptism is how Christians profess their faith; it's how **we publicly identify with Jesus.** It's how we say to the watching world, 'I'm connected to Jesus. I'm one of His followers. I'm on his team.'

ILLUSTRATION

In sports, people represent their team by wearing a jersey. Cristiano Ronaldo wears Portugal's jersey. Tom Brady wears the Patriots' jersey. And when a Christian gets baptized, he (or she) is putting on the jersey to identify with team Jesus.[2] And more than that, when Christians get baptized, they act out what has happened to them spiritually. As a new Christian goes

2 I got this illustration of a jersey from Egghead, Jonathan Leeman.

down in the water, he shows how he has, in a sense, died. As he comes up from the water, he shows how in Jesus, he's a new person with new life. 'The old has passed away, behold, the new has come' (2 Cor. 5:17; Rom. 6:3-4)

Being baptized is one of the first acts of obedience for a Christian. It's a one-time act for Christians, not to be repeated. So, if you're a Christian but you haven't been baptized, talk to your pastor. If you have been baptized, do the work of trying to see others baptized (we'll talk about that more in the next chapter).

3. At church, God's meal is eaten. (1 Cor. 11) The Lord's Supper, what's often called communion, is a meal Jesus commanded Christians to eat in order to remember Him and His death (1 Cor. 11:24-26). The meal reflects the love and unity among God's people, not selfishness and division.

In 1 Corinthians 11, Paul corrects a local church. They thought they were gathering for the Lord's Supper, but they actually weren't. Why? Because these Corinthian Christians used the Lord's Supper to stuff themselves with food and alcohol. They weren't waiting on each other to show up or looking out for one another; they were just looking out for themselves.

God's meal wasn't meant for this. Rather it was meant for us to be strengthened in our faith, to examine ourselves, remember Christ's death, and proclaim that He's coming again. So as Jason prepares for the Lord's Supper, he should make sure his relationship with the Lord and with others is right. Yet he also should look forward to the day the Lord is coming back, and enjoy the supper as a taste of the supper that we'll enjoy with Jesus one day (Rev. 19:6-9).

4. At Church, God's praises are sung (Eph. 5:18-19). Considering how the Corinthian Christians were treating one another, it's no surprise that Paul tells Christians not to get drunk.

Instead, he commands us to 'be filled with the Spirit, addressing one another in psalms and hymns and spiritual songs, singing and making melody to the Lord with your heart' (Eph. 5:18–19).

Have you ever considered singing as part of how you obey Jesus? The most repeated command in the Bible is the command to sing! Too often, Christians avoid singing because they don't like the songs or they can't sing well. But our Savior, not our likes or our skills, should determine how loud we raise our voices. Ever since Jesus' empty tomb, there's been a lot to sing about. Let's not forget that one of the primary reasons we go to church is to encourage other Christians, and one of the primary ways we do this is through singing.

5. At church, God's people pray (Eph. 5:20). Paul also commands the church to give 'thanks always and for everything to God the Father in the name of our Lord Jesus Christ.'

In Acts 2:42, we saw that the early church was 'devoted...to the prayers.' God's gathered people are a praying people. While individual prayer is wonderful, there's something about praying together with other Christians.

This kind of prayer helps us to remember others' interests (Phil. 2:4).

This kind of prayer reflects our unity.

Praying together with other Christians shows that we understand our connection to one another through Jesus. Remember, the Lord's Prayer begins with '*Our* Father,' not '*My* Father.'

ILLUSTRATION

At my church, a white, elderly sister, who grew up in a society that told her to never associate with black people, prayed with a young, black brother about his ministry efforts at a historically black university. They're members of the same church, and more importantly, members of the same body—Jesus' body. Her prayers for him showed that his concerns were hers. No walls the world wanted to put up could divide them. So together, they went before their heavenly Father with their requests. This little scene is like a dress rehearsal of the great day when Christians from every tribe and tongue are gathered together.

So, if your church prays together, join in on those prayers. Say 'amen,' and say it loudly. When we say, 'amen,' we're saying, 'I agree with that prayer; that's my prayer, too.'

STOP:

Which of these five activities do you appreciate most? Why?

Together, Christians

hear God's Word,

baptize those who believe,

eat God's meal,

sing God's praises,

and pray.

How can Jason get involved in these things? Here are three suggestions so simple any Christian can do them.

HOW CAN YOU LOVE YOUR FAMILY?

ATTEND REGULARLY | The first, most basic way Jason can love his church is by attending regularly. Hershael York described this first step well:

> The easiest act of obedience for a Christian is gathering with the church for worship on Sunday. It only requires that

> you get up, get dressed, and get there. Yet, amazingly, many Christians today will not do the easiest thing, and wonder why they struggle with the difficult things.[3]

Did you know God commands Christians to regularly gather with a local church? In Hebrews 10:24-25, God says, 'Let us consider how to stir up one another to love and good works, *not neglecting to meet together,* as is the habit of some, but encouraging one another.'

Of course, there will be times where we're sick or out of town, but overall, people should be able to count on us to gather with the church. *The most basic ministry we have is the ministry of simply showing up.*

Some Christians say they don't need a church to encourage other Christians; they can do that with their Christian friends. But if they don't go to church, how will they take part in the five things we just thought about? To not join in on those things is sinful, and if their group of friends is doing all five of those things, then they're probably more of a church than not. Pastor Mark Dever's advice here is helpful because it connects loving people at church with the two great commandments, which we looked at in Chapter One:

> The church is what puts steel in the spine of Jesus' command to love your neighbor as yourself and love the Lord your God. Until someone understands the church, you're really only talking about someone choosing to love their friends, and even unbelievers do that (Luke 6:33). It's the church that gives those commands a Jesus-like shape because it's the

3 Hershael York, <https://twitter.com/hershaelyork/status/934743300485140481>. Date accessed: 5th July 2019.

> church where all types of people, who would be enemies in the world, are gathered together.[4]

If you're a Christian and reading this but you've been neglecting church, I have good news for you: there is grace for you to be forgiven. Let this grace encourage you to start going to church regularly. *Everyone at any church is just as broken as you are, and needs just as much grace as you.* Satan would love to shame you out of going to church, but don't let him. See what churches are around you, find one that preaches the good news of Jesus, and love your brothers and sisters by regularly attending their gatherings.

JOIN QUICKLY | Attending church is a good step in love, but it's not the final step. After all, going to church doesn't make you a Christian any more than standing in a garage makes you a car. If you are a Christian and your church offers membership, and I hope it does, you should love them by *joining* your church as a member.

If we say we belong to *the universal Church* without belonging to *a local church,* we sound like someone who says they're a baseball player but they're not on a team. That just doesn't make sense. The Bible lays out an expectation that we join local churches. In 1 Corinthians 5, Paul says *there's an inside and an outside to the local church.* How can we know the difference? *Church membership is the answer.*

Earlier in this chapter, we talked about a church's family life. Many Christians miss out on the joy and beauty of this because they don't commit to one church. A guy who goes on many dates with many gals may have fun, but he'll never experience the deep love that marriage offers. What's more, he's clearly bent on what he can get out of relationships, not what he can give to them.

---

4 Mark Dever said this to me in a personal conversation.

Likewise, those who 'date' lots of churches but don't commit to one will never experience the depth of love that a local church has to offer.[5] *To be a Christian is to be someone who isn't looking to be served but to serve,* which brings us to our last suggestion.

SERVE FAITHFULLY | In Mark 10:43-45, Jesus said that the greatest among us would be a servant. Jason can love his church by faithfully serving it. By 'faithfully serving,' I simply mean that people can trust Jason to help in whatever ways he can. There are plenty of ways for him to help. He doesn't need to wait until he feels like he's 'gifted' in a certain area, and he certainly shouldn't demand to serve only where and when he wants. If he did that, it would show his service is more about him than those he's serving. But if Jason is happy to meet any need—like setting out chairs—then he'll have lots of opportunities to serve.

So how specifically can Jason serve his church? If you read the New Testament and circle the phrase 'one another,' you'll soon have lots of circles on the pages of your Bible. All of those are invitations to joyful obedience. But let me highlight two commands that all Christians can obey to serve their local church.

First, you can **practice hospitality** (1 Pet. 4:9). Have people over to your home, apartment, or dorm room. In Acts 2, we read, 'Day by day, attending the temple together and breaking bread *in their homes,* they received their food with glad and generous hearts.' I love how this verse connects hospitality with the heart. Hospitality is a heart issue, not a space issue. A college student who invites a family of five to his dorm room for dinner gets this point. So, even if it's small, have people over to your home.

The second way you can faithfully serve your church is to **disciple someone,** which simply means to help someone follow Jesus. In

---

5 Of course, joining a church does not bind you to that church like marriage binds you to another person!

Matthew 28, Jesus says that to be a disciple is to be someone who makes disciples. While all church members do this in informal ways, find someone whom you can regularly meet with and help each other follow Jesus. While it's great if this person is older than you, they don't need to be older. Typically, however, it helps if this person is the same gender as you.

JASON

The church service ended, and Jason was about to go help Eddy clean up the chairs when old Ms. Pearl grabbed the tail of his shirt. She was kind of crazy, at least in Jason's mind, but he was realizing that she was his kind-of-crazy grandma in Christ. That made him wait to hear what she had to say.

She let the room clear a bit before she spoke.

'You know I knew your father, child,' Ms. Pearl said calmly. She shook her head with a sad expression. 'I'm so sorry for what he did.'

Jason was shocked by what she said—mainly because it made sense.

'Oh, um, yeah,' Jason said as he fumbled about, looking for the right words. 'He had issues.'

'True,' Ms. Pearl responded as she sat back. Her tone was as sweet as her response was short, despite Jason saying something as obvious as the color of the sky.

'He also had something else.'

'What's that?' Jason asked with curiosity. What was Ms. Pearl about to reveal—that Jason's dad had another family? That he had a criminal record?

'Regret,' Ms. Pearl said.

Jason expected Ms. Pearl to say a lot of things, but not that.

'Ms. Pearl, I—'

'Child, your daddy's feeling bad don't justify nothing he's done. No ifs, ands, or buts about it. But I just thought it might help you to know that he wasn't happy about a thing he did to your family, seeing as the preacher preached on Jesus' compassion and all that. Your daddy was talking to me some years ago when I saw him last, and he had more regret than a pig did bacon.'

Jason didn't know whether to cry or laugh, but he hung in there, trying to understand.

'Anyhow, I know what he did hurt you real bad, you and your Mom, and that makes all the sense in the world, baby. What's helped me is to remember that in this sinful world, some things just gon' stay broke.'

Jason seemed confused. Was this supposed to be encouraging? Ms. Pearl saw Jason's confusion and tried to clarify what she meant.

'What I mean, baby, is there are some wounds that only the resurrection can heal. But Jesus gon' heal us good, child, heal us all the way 'til we're better than new. Every tear he'll wipe. Preacher said Jesus promised us that much.'

'Thank you, Ms. Pearl,' Jason said. 'I'm honestly not sure what to say.'

'That's OK, baby! You get on and help Eddy with them chairs cause they ain't gon' fold themselves,' Ms. Pearl said with a wink.

'Yes, Ms. Pearl,' Jason said, now smiling.

Jason helped his brother Eddy fold chairs. He realized what a basic task he was doing, in a place that seemed to be filled with so many ordinary, kooky people. At the same time, Jason was in awe of this new family God gave him in this little local church. But most surprising of all, he knew he was growing to love them as they loved him, as God loved them.

MEMORY VERSE

'Let us consider how to stir up one another to love and good works, not neglecting to meet together, as is the habit of some, but encouraging one another, and all the more as you see the Day approaching.' (Heb. 10:24-25)

SUMMARY

In this chapter, we learned about the universal church and the local church. At church, God's Word is preached and believed, and believers are baptized. At church, God's meal is eaten and His praises are sung. What's more, at church God's people pray. So disciples should regularly attend, join, and serve a church.

WHAT'S THE POINT?

Followers of Jesus share the gospel with people who don't know Jesus.

7. EVANGELISM: LOVING THE LOST

JASON

Jason sat with Eddy as they met up for dinner, and Eddy stared at the menu.

'The chicken sounds really good, but—'

'I just hate it,' Jason said, cutting Eddy off.

'It's that bad, huh?' Eddy asked.

'What? No!' Jason said. 'I hate that Al and Chip don't know Jesus.'

'Ah,' Eddy said, realizing they were diving deep before they'd even ordered their food. 'Tell me more.' He laid his menu aside.

As the two talked, Jason realized just how badly he wanted Al and Chip to know God.

'Your sadness over your friends isn't a bad thing,' Eddy said. He reminded Jason that the apostle Paul wasn't OK with people rejecting God either. 'In Romans 9, Paul talks about "great sorrow" and "unceasing anguish" he had because people who were like him didn't know Jesus.'

He continued, 'Knowing that people you love don't love Jesus, well, it causes a sadness that doesn't really end for Christians—not in this life at least.'

'But there's got to be something—anything—I can do?' Jason asked.

'Well, yes,' said Eddy, 'you can evangelize them.'

'Huh? Evan-jelly?' Jason asked, as if Eddy had spoken another language. 'What does jelly have to do with this? I'm talking about my friends' souls and you keep talking about food!'

Eddy put on a gentle smile and answered his young friend slowly.

'I mean you can share the gospel with them, brother. That's what you can do.'

STOP:

How did you first hear the gospel?

In this last chapter, we looked at Jason's church and saw what the Bible says about how Christians love other Christians.

God also calls Christians to love non-Christians, which *has more to do with the church than you might think*. We saw in Chapter One how Christians should love their neighbor, whoever that neighbor may be. Galatians 6:10 commands Christians to especially care for people in their church, but it also says Christians should do good to everyone. Genesis 1:26–28 tells us that *every person is made in God's image,* which means *every person is a special creation* made to show what God is like. *Every person is worthy of love.* And so Jason wants to share the gospel with his friends.

But how? How would he tell them? Should he tell them about Jesus, or is it just his pastor's job?

In this chapter, we're going to look at what the Bible says about evangelism and how Christians should evangelize. This is the last topic in our public training, one that can make the difference between heaven and hell.

WHAT IS EVANGELISM?

According to the Bible, evangelism is *sharing the gospel with unbelievers with the hope they'll repent of their sins and trust in Christ*. It's part of every Christian's job description.

Let's walk through this definition. Evangelism is…

Sharing the gospel | After talking about his great sorrow, Paul asks an important question in Romans 10: How will someone get saved if they don't hear the gospel? The gospel is a message. We'll make sure we've got that message right later in this chapter. But for now, we need to understand that evangelism is sharing a specific message, *the gospel message*. At the root of the word 'Evangelism' is 'evangel,' which is a Greek word for gospel. (Much of the Bible was originally written in Greek.) The word 'gospel' literally means *good news*. In ancient times, a soldier would run back from battle with news of victory; he would return with a gospel message. And through His death and resurrection, Jesus has conquered death for all who trust in Him. That's the heart of the biblical gospel.

With unbelievers | Unless we're talking to ourselves, we'll be sharing this message with someone. It's great to preach the gospel to yourself, and it's encouraging to remind your Christian brothers and sisters of the gospel. But these audiences don't make for evangelism. In Luke 15, Jesus uses a word to describe those who don't trust in Him: He says they are *lost*. They don't know where they're going even if they think they do, and so *we evangelize by sharing the gospel message with the lost*.

With the hope that they will repent of their sins and trust in Christ | We share the gospel message with the lost not to show how holy we are, or to check off a box on a spiritual to-do list. We share the gospel with the lost so that *they may be found!* What's the point of giving someone a map if you don't want them to know where to go? Evangelism is telling someone the best news *in hopes of leading them away* from the worst place, hell. And *so we evangelize with the hope of seeing people turn from sin and trust in Jesus.*

And it's a part of every Christian's job description. | Evangelism is a part of what it means to be a Christian. It's not just for pastors, extroverts, or really serious Christians. Jesus commanded all Christians to make disciples (Matt. 28:20). We know that command includes us because in the same verse, Jesus promised to be with us 'until the end of the age.' Jesus is with us by His Spirit, the Holy Spirit, which comes to live in us when we trust in Jesus. The Spirit is going to be a major factor in our evangelism, as we'll see soon. But first, we have to understand that since Jesus hasn't come back yet, there's still evangelistic work left for us to do.

Evangelism
[ih-van-juh-liz-uh m]

noun

1. The sharing of the gospel with unbelievers with the hope that they will repent of their sins and trust in Christ; a part of every Christian's job description.

So, you may work as a farmer, lawyer, mother, or construction worker, but if you're a Christian, **your work is also to share the gospel with the lost**. It's to be a witness (Acts 1:8), an evangelist. Evangelism isn't all we do as Christians, but it shouldn't be something we never do. Every Christian should regularly evangelize.

But maybe, like Jason, you're unsure how to evangelize. That's OK. Or maybe you're a Christian reading this, and you're saddened because you haven't been sharing the gospel. Maybe you've been sinfully silent.

Here's the good news: We can confess our lack of evangelism to God, and enjoy the grace of His forgiveness. Our hope isn't that we share the gospel perfectly, but that *we trust in a perfect gospel.* God's grace is ultimately what will motivate us to share the gospel. Guilt may motivate us for a while, but that motivation won't last. Instead, when we know the freedom of God's forgiveness, we want to tell others of that forgiveness.

But what *is* the message of forgiveness? Let's make sure we've got the gospel right, before we get to how it's shared.

GETTING THE MESSAGE RIGHT: WHAT IS THE GOSPEL?

We've thought about the gospel throughout this book, but let's make sure we know a way to quickly sum it up. If we can do that, we'll be better evangelists. There are many ways to rightly present the gospel, but a simple summary takes four words: God, Man, Christ, Response.

God → *Man* → *Christ* → *Response*

The gospel is good news about God. It's His message. God made everything, and it was good; after He made mankind, everything was *very* good (Gen. 1:31). He made people to rule the earth and fill it with people who would obey and worship Him. If we don't know these basic facts, we won't understand the rest of the gospel. If we don't know that God is good, we won't grasp why sin is bad. If we don't appreciate how the world was made, we won't understand how we made it a mess. This leads to our next point: Man.

God → **Man** → *Christ* → *Response*

Though God was a good king, Adam and Eve rebelled against him. Since Adam represented us before God, when he sinned, we sinned along with him. That **sin brought about a curse on the rest of the world**; all creation is now frustrated (Romans 8:22). Work is spoiled. Relationships are broken—vertically, between God and people, and horizontally, between people and people.

All people are now born as sinners,

and deserve death

and eternal separation from God,

suffering under his holy wrath (Ps. 51; Rom. 3).

But praise God, Jesus came.

God → *Man* → **Christ** → *Response*

Jesus is God, the eternal Son of God the Father. He became a man to live the life we should have lived, perfectly obeying God. He died the death sinners deserved on the cross, and He was raised three days later from the dead. Just as death and sin came to us through Adam, eternal life comes to all who trust in Jesus (Rom. 5). After he was raised from the dead, Jesus went up to heaven and now reigns with God, and He will come again to finally bring His people home. When He does, we'll enjoy a new world, one even better than the original we messed up. But *God's enemies will be cast away to suffer forever in hell.*

God → *Man* → *Christ* → **Response**

The gospel demands a response. We either trust in this gospel or turn away from it—there's no neutral option. We should make this clear to the people we evangelize. We shouldn't tell them about God, Man, and Christ and let them think that's one of many nice religious options out there. Rather, we should invite them to trust in Christ, the only way to God (John 14:6). We should even plead with people to do so (2 Cor. 5:20). As J.I. Packer wrote, '[Evangelizing] is a matter, not merely of informing, but also of inviting.'[1] The gospel is only good news for those who believe it. When Jesus announced the gospel, it came with a required response: 'Repent and believe' (Mark 1:15).

So we've got the gospel. But how do we share it? What follows are biblical principles to guide our evangelism.

SHARING THE MESSAGE RIGHT: HOW DO I SHARE THE GOSPEL?

Lots of things are mistaken as evangelism. So we need to clarify what we're talking about. We can say it is *not this, but that...*

Not This: A Testimony

When we share the gospel, we're not talking about sharing your testimony. A testimony is a Christian's story of how they became a Christian. For a biblical example of a testimony, look at how Paul talks about the change in his life in Philippians 3 or Acts 22.

Some Christians have dramatic testimonies because they lived so clearly against God, and He saved them through incredible ways. If you're one of these Christians, when you write out your testimony, talk discreetly about your sin before you met Jesus. Some Christians, often with the best of intentions, graphically describe their sin to show the lengths God went to save them. *But people don't need to know all the gory details to know that you were a great sinner and that God is a great Savior.* So you don't need to recount them all (Eph. 5:12).

---

1 J. I. Packer, *Sovereignty of God* (Downers Grove, IL: InterVarsity, 2008), p. 53.

JASON

Jason remembered that when he used to run his mouth as a child, Ms. Pearl would tell him: 'Child, you don't have to say everything you know.' We'd do well to take her wisdom.

Some other Christians say they have 'boring testimonies,' the kind every Christian parent wants their kids to have. These Christians don't remember *not* trusting in Christ. If you're one of these Christians, *be careful not to downplay God's work in your life*. He has given you a new heart, and kept that heart from straying for so long! All Christians have a story to tell of God's amazing grace in their lives.

STOP:

Have you written out your testimony before and shared it with someone? Is there someone you could share your story with? If you've never written it out, do so. Describe what your life was like before you knew Jesus, and how your life has changed since.

But That: Telling God's Story

Though our stories may be great, God's story is greater. Sharing our testimonies is wonderful, but sharing them with someone isn't the same thing as sharing the gospel. In my part of the world, people are happy for anything to give anyone a sense of direction or purpose in life. Folks wouldn't care if I said it was my living room lamp that got me going. But when we share with someone that they're also a rebel who needs to repent, that's when we are coming full circle with our evangelism.

Not This: Apologetics, Guilt-Tripping, or Magic-Tricking

When we share the gospel, we're also not talking about defending the gospel. That's called apologetics, and it's often the conversation that follows sharing the gospel. Apologetics is wonderful, and we're called to defend our faith (1 Pet. 3:15). But defending the gospel and sharing the gospel isn't the same thing.

What's more, *when we share the gospel, we're not simply trying to make people feel bad for their sins.* **The Holy Spirit brings conviction; we can't.** Neither can we convince someone of the gospel with a particular method. Someone trusting in Jesus is not ultimately up to us! This should ultimately encourage us in evangelism.

So, when we're talking about evangelism, we're not talking about a solo project, as if it's all up to us, or a way to spin the gospel just right.

Some people are saved after hearing the gospel once;

some people are saved after hearing it a bunch of times.

Some are saved by hearing sermons;

some are saved after a bunch of conversations with a friend.

There's no magic way to convince someone of the truth of the gospel.

But That: Faithful Seed-Sowing

Our job is to plant the seed and let God give the growth (1 Cor. 3:6). We share the message of God's grace as people who have experienced that grace. We share as humble, compassionate, and joyful evangelists who trust that it's God who saves.

Evangelism requires God, but it also can involve our brothers and sisters. In the previous chapter, we looked at why church is so important for Christians. We didn't talk about the church's evangelistic purpose, and I don't mean its role in paying for missionaries and sending them around the world, though churches should do that. I'm talking about how **God says** that our love for other Christians will show the world that we're Jesus' disciples (John 13:35). I'm talking about how **God says** that Christians' unity with one another will teach others about Jesus (John 17:20). I'm talking about how **God commands** His people to live such holy lives that non-believers have reason to praise God when He returns (1 Pet. 2:12).

This doesn't mean that we 'preach the gospel, and if necessary we use words' as some people say. **The gospel *is* words,** and **there's no gospel without words.** But if we're trying to share the gospel without love for our brothers and sisters, then we're robbing ourselves of one of the most powerful pictures God uses to teach non-Christians about Himself. Where else can people clearly see love, unity, and holiness among Christians?

JASON

'That's exactly what's happening with Chip!' Jason told Eddy. 'He's seeing our friendship, and it's showing him what God is like. He's seeing that we're disciples!'

'Praise God,' Eddy said, with his warm smile. 'Why not share the gospel with him so he can become a disciple, too? And that other friend of yours, Al, remind me—is he a Christian?'

'Al's my brother,' Jason said, 'like, my blood brother. But yeah, as a kid he called himself a Christian. But the older he got, the more he seemed to love sin. Unlike Chip, Al has been anything but interested in the gospel.'

'Ah, gotcha,' Eddy said, shaking his head. 'Makes me think of Demas.'

'Who?' Jason asked.

'One of the Apostle Paul's friends who ditched him. Paul said he 'was in love with the present world.' How's that for something to read on your tombstone?'

'I hope Al's reads something different.' Jason paused for a moment. 'Hey, earlier we talked about sorrow that doesn't go away. There's really nothing I can do about that?'

Eddy explained to Jason that while Christians never want to just stop caring about someone's spiritual state, we can make peace with the fact that we can't do anything more to persuade some folks.

'Our hope isn't in the results of our evangelism,' Eddy said. 'It's that God is good and right in all that He does, and that His plans are better than ours. And we should remain hopeful! Our sorrow will be gone in heaven, and who knows what God might do with the seeds we sow until then? There was one pastor who said, "The seed [we plant] may lie under the earth till we lie there, *and then spring up!*"'[2]

'You're getting all poetic on me now,' Jason said.

Eddy laughed. 'Well, let me try another picture then. When it comes to evangelism, some of us are the ones planting the seed, some of us are the ones watering the seed, and some of us are the ones seeing the harvest. But here's the thing—none of us have a bird's eye view of God's garden. Some of us may feel like we're pulling weeds and some of us may see things bloom, but we're all in the work together.'

Eddy went on to explain that wanting to see fruit from our evangelism is a good thing. John 15 says we'll bear fruit if we're

---

2 Charles Bridges, *The Christian Ministry* (Carlisle, PA: Banner of Truth, 2009), p. 75.

trusting in Jesus. But it never promises that fruit will be people trusting in Him because of our evangelism. Nonetheless, Eddy explained to Jason that what matters is faithfulness, not results. He encouraged Jason to marvel that God would even use him to share the best news in the world (2 Cor. 5:20). He encouraged Jason to see how evangelism is a wonderful privilege but a horrible burden if we think the entire weight of someone's salvation rests on us. Jason and Eddy talked about times Paul was discouraged in his evangelism, and how God even used lousy evangelists like Jonah. They talked about getting rejected in their evangelism, and temptations that come from not wanting to be rejected.

'It's tempting to do something that always gets a response. Some people will even change the gospel so it's easier to swallow,' Eddy said to Jason. 'But know this, brother, if we change the gospel, we lose it. When you're tempted to switch things up so evangelism feels easier, that's when you have to decide whether or not you'll stay faithful.'

'But what if Chip asks me about stuff I don't know?'

'What if!' said Eddy. 'Jason, just because you don't know everything doesn't mean you don't know anything. You know the gospel, and you can always tell him you'll look into something and get back to him. So even if you're scared, trust God and tell him the gospel. Moses was scared to give the message God gave him, but look what God did.'

'I like that—not asking, "what if" but saying "even if." Is that in the Bible?'

'Nope. That's just wise old Eddy.'

'Oh, kill me now,' Jason said.

Jason knew one day the sadness he felt for his friends would end, but until then, he would train to love God and his neighbors.

MEMORY VERSE

'I planted, Apollos watered, but God gave the growth.' (1 Cor. 3:6)

SUMMARY

In this chapter, we learned about a major part of every Christian's job description—evangelism. Evangelism is sharing the gospel with unbelievers with the hope they'll repent of their sins and trust in Jesus Christ. The gospel message can be summed up in four words: God, Man, Christ, Response—and when we talk about sharing it, we're not talking about *this* tip or trick but *that* faithful presentation.

CONCLUSION: NEVER RECOVER!

A Christian doctor once ran his race well. But even more importantly, he finished it well. Martyn Lloyd-Jones was his name, and his daughter, Lady Catherwood, adored him. When asked why her father's ministry was so effective, she gave this answer:

'He never recovered from the fact that God saved him.'

Don't miss the happy irony—the doctor didn't know how to recover. God had healed him of spiritual sickness, turned him from a hostile enemy into a royal son. This never became just another event in the doctor's life, like receiving a thank you card or graduating from one grade to the next. Simply put, the gift of salvation colored the doctor's whole life. Though God graciously granted it to him, the doctor never took salvation for granted.

May we, by God's grace, see our Christian faith this way. May we never recover from God's saving work in our lives. May we stumble into heaven still reeling from having been saved. No doubt, while here on earth, we'll have sour seasons of life, where salvation doesn't seem all that sweet. But let's pray we always savor something of its flavor in our hearts. Let's always work, by God's grace, to taste and see that the Lord is good. Let's work to keep enjoying the basics of the Christian life—loving God and neighbor, hearing from God through His Word, speaking to God in prayer, worshiping God with our lives, encouraging our brothers and sisters at church, and sharing the gospel with the lost. After all, brothers and sisters, we never graduate from the basics, and the second we think we have is the second we prove we haven't. Of course, there's a wrong way to hear that story about the thankful and effective doctor. The point we should take is that God's grace ought to amaze us, not how effective we can be on His behalf. The point of this book is to know and enjoy God's grace more and see how the spiritual disciplines help us to do so.

Our goal isn't effectiveness or perfection. Our goal is simply to know Jesus, and to join in His sufferings, becoming like Him in His death, that by any means we may attain the resurrection of the dead (Phil. 3:8-11). So, may we finish the race. May we fight the good fight. May we make it home to heaven and be amazed that we're even there.

'My soul makes its boast in the LORD,' says Psalm 34:2. And may the one who boasts boast in this—that he knows God.

Brothers and sisters, may we grow to know Him.

And may we never recover.

'For the grace of God has appeared, bringing salvation for all people, ***training*** *us to renounce ungodliness and worldly passions, and to live self-controlled, upright, and godly lives in the present age, waiting for our blessed hope, the appearing of the glory of our great God and Savior Jesus Christ, who gave himself for us to redeem us from all lawlessness and to purify for himself a people for his own possession who are zealous for good works.'* (Titus 2:11-14)

This series of short workbooks, from the 9Marks series, are designed to help you think through some of life's big questions.

1. GOD: Is He Out There?
2. WAR: Why Did Life Just Get Harder?
3. VOICES: Who Am I Listening To?
4. BIBLE: Can We Trust It?
5. BELIEVE: What Should I Know?
6. CHARACTER: How Do I Change?
7. TRAINING: How Do I Grow As A Christian?
8. CHURCH: Do I Have To Go?
9. RELATIONSHIPS: How Do I Make Things Right?
10. SERVICE: How Do I Give Back?

Building Healthy Churches

9Marks exists to equip church leaders with a biblical vision and practical resources for displaying God's glory to the nations through healthy churches.

To that end, we want to see churches characterized by these nine marks of health:

1 Expositional Preaching
2 Biblical Theology
3 A Biblical Understanding of the Gospel
4 A Biblical Understanding of Conversion
5 A Biblical Understanding of Evangelism
6 Biblical Church Membership
7 Biblical Church Discipline
8 Biblical Discipleship
9 Biblical Church Leadership

Christian Focus Publications

Our mission statement —

STAYING FAITHFUL

In dependence upon God we seek to impact the world through literature faithful to His infallible Word, the Bible. Our aim is to ensure that the Lord Jesus Christ is presented as the only hope to obtain forgiveness of sin, live a useful life and look forward to heaven with Him.

Our books are published in four imprints:

CHRISTIAN FOCUS

Popular works including biographies, commentaries, basic doctrine and Christian living.

CHRISTIAN HERITAGE

Books representing some of the best material from the rich heritage of the church.

MENTOR

Books written at a level suitable for Bible College and seminary students, pastors, and other serious readers. The imprint includes commentaries, doctrinal studies, examination of current issues and church history.

CF4•K

Children's books for quality Bible teaching and for all age groups: Sunday school curriculum, puzzle and activity books; personal and family devotional titles, biographies and inspirational stories — because you are never too young to know Jesus!

Christian Focus Publications Ltd,
Geanies House, Fearn, Ross-shire,
IV20 1TW, Scotland, United Kingdom.
www.christianfocus.com